Think Twice
Teacher's Book

Think Twice

Communication activities for
beginner to intermediate students

Teacher's Book

David Hover

The right of the
University of Cambridge
to print and sell
all manner of books
was granted by
Henry VIII in 1534.
The University has printed
and published continuously
since 1584.

Cambridge University Press
Cambridge
New York   Port Chester
Melbourne   Sydney

Published by the Press Syndicate of the University of Cambridge
The Pitt Building, Trumpington Street, Cambridge CB2 1RP
32 East 57th Street, New York, NY 10022, USA
10 Stamford Road, Oakleigh, Melbourne 3166, Australia

© Cambridge University Press 1986

First published 1986
Third printing 1989

Printed in Great Britain at The Bath Press, Avon

ISBN 0 521 27386 2 Teacher's Book
ISBN 0 521 27385 4 Student's Book

CONTENTS

Introduction

1 The basic principles   1

  1.1   Each activity practises a structure or function   1
  1.2   The activities are communicative   1
  1.3   The students work independently of the teacher   1
  1.4   The material for each activity is realistic   1

2 Using the activities in class   2

  2.1   The format of the Student's Book   2
  2.2   Preparing for an activity   2
     Familiarizing the students with the situation and the task(s)
     Preparing and practising the language needed for the activity
  2.3   The activity itself   2
  2.4   Classroom organization   3
     Seating
     Large classes
     The third student
     Private lessons

3 Fitting the activity into your teaching programme   3

  3.1   Each activity is independent of the others   3
  3.2   How competent the students should be in the language needed for an activity before they attempt it   3
  3.3   Beginner or Intermediate? The minimum level for an activity   4
  3.4   Using the activities at higher levels   4
  3.5   Progressive use of the activities   4
     Getting used to a new approach
     Acquiring skills

4 Note on scanning   5

  4.1   How to teach scanning   5
  4.2   The reading passages in the Student's Book   5
  4.3   Student resistance to scanning   5

5 The headings in the Teacher's Notes for each activity   6

  5.1   Notes and Ideas   6
  5.2   Aim   6
  5.3   Situation   6
  5.4   Structures   6
  5.5   Lexis   6
  5.6   Setting Up   7
  5.7   Monitoring   7

v

Contents

5.8   Solution   7
5.9   Homework   7
5.10   Preparation Activities   7
5.11   Follow Up   7
5.12   Role-play (with video)   7

6   **General Teaching Notes and Ideas**   8

6.1   Teaching the language needed for an activity   8
6.2   Note-taking   8
6.3   Simple communicative exercises   8
6.4   Setting-up alternatives   10
6.5   Monitoring   10
        Intervening
        Monitoring Check List
6.6   Leading follow-up discussions with low-level students   11
6.7   Video   11
        The improvisation
        Adapting the improvisations for a tape recorder
        Using video improvisations to set up an activity
6.8   Using the activities with mixed-level classes   12

7   **If the activity goes badly: Check List**   12

8   **Abbreviations, etc. used in the Student's and Teacher's Books**   12

Notes and Ideas for the activities

(For notes to *Introduction to scanning* (Student's Book, p. 9), see section 4.1 in the Introduction, above.)

UNIT 1   **personal identity (name, address, etc.); the alphabet; numbers**

1   **Missing!**   13
    to be (third person)

2   **The Social Security**   16
    to be (third person)

3   **Business cards**   18
    to be and Simple Present (third person)

4   **Holiday photos**   20
    to be; possessives; family relations

5   **The delivery man**   22
    numbers; correcting facts

Contents

UNIT 2 *there is/are*; simple adjectives of places and people; *have (got)*; *can*; *like*

6 **Holiday hotels** 24
   there is/are versus *it is/they are*

7 **Advertisements** 26
   giving opinions on how people look; *too*

8 **Exchanges** 28
   have (got); *to want* (third person)

9 **Traffic signs** 30
   can (permission); giving directions

10 **Love-match** 32
   can (ability); *to like* (third person)

UNIT 3 *how old/tall?*, etc.; *how much/many?*; directions; prepositions; the weather

11 **Calories** 34
   height, weight, age and other quantities

12 **Recipes** 37
   how much? versus *how many?*; *to need*; *have (got)*

13 **Lost in Spa** 39
   prepositions and giving directions

14 **Stage plan** 42
   prepositions and describing furniture

15 **The weather** 45
   describing the weather; agreeing and disagreeing

UNIT 4 the Simple Present

16 **Timetables** 47
   Simple Present (opening times)

17 **Neighbours** 50
   Simple Present (habitual actions)

18 **The Housing Committee** 52
   Simple Present (identity); *to want*; *to need*; *there is/are*

19 **Health quiz** 55
   Simple Present (frequency adverbs, habitual actions)

20 **Star signs** 57
   Simple Present (likes/dislikes, habitual actions); *to be*

UNIT 5 the Present Continuous and *going to*

21 **The department store** 60
   Present Continuous (present actions); telling the time

22 **Introductions** 63
   Present Continuous versus Simple Present

Contents

23 **Greek holidays** 65
making plans (*shall we?*) and talking about plans (*going to*)

24 **The dinner party** 68
talking about plans (*going to* or Present Continuous as future)

25 **At the cinema** 70
Present Continuous (talking about a picture) versus Simple Present (outlining a scenario); *going to* (predictions and plans)

UNIT 6 the Simple Past and the Past Continuous

26 **Language school** 73
to be (present versus past)

27 **The class of '76** 76
Simple Past (*Yes/No* questions) versus Simple Present

28 **The seminar** 78
Simple Past (*Wh* questions)

29 **Car hire** 81
Past Continuous and describing people

30 **Public lives** 84
Simple Past (dates of birth/death, etc.)

UNIT 7 *must; have to; had to;* question tags

31 **Business letters** 86
must (telling someone the correct way of doing something)

32 **Business trip** 88
have (got) to versus *would like to*

33 **Au pairs** 91
have (got) to versus *had to*

34 **Second opinions** 94
question tags and *Wh* questions

UNIT 8 the Present Perfect and the Present Perfect Continuous

35 **Interviews** 97
Present Perfect (with *ever*: talking about experience) versus Simple Past

36 **Soap opera** 100
Present Perfect (recent events)

37 **Politics** 102
Present Perfect (finished and unfinished periods)

38 **Getting in touch** 105
Present Perfect Continuous and Simple Past

39 **The Nenebridge Reporter** 108
revision of tenses and some Passive

Introduction

1 The basic principles

The activities in *Think Twice* are for adult students of English at beginner and intermediate levels. They are intended to complement the average teaching programme at these levels, and require minimal preparation or additional teaching. They are for classroom use and each takes approximately twenty to thirty minutes of class time to complete.

The basic elements in each activity are as follows:

1.1 Each activity practises a structure or function

The students only need to know one or two structures to be able to do a particular activity. Accordingly, once they have learned a particular structure, you can give them the corresponding activity for further practice or consolidation.

The structures and functions for each activity are outlined in the Contents, and given in detail under Aim and Structures in the teacher's notes for each activity.

(see also section 3.2)

1.2 The activities are communicative

In each activity the students are given a task. Since the information they need for the task is split into two parts (Student A and Student B), no student has enough information to be able to do it alone. Accordingly, the students have to ask each other for the information they need and come to a decision together.

In this sense, the activities are not exercises, but contexts in which the students can use language to find out about things they genuinely need to know and to share ideas.

(see also sections 3.2 and 6.3)

1.3 The students work independently of the teacher

The material for each activity is self-sufficient, so that once the students fully understand what they have to do, they should be left to work entirely independently.

For the students, this will give them experience of the kind of problems they will meet outside a controlled classroom situation, and teach them to cope and take initiatives by themselves.

For you, the teacher, it will give you an idea of the problems which the students have in communicating without your support, and of how well they have mastered the language you have taught them.

(see also section 6.5)

1.4 The material for each activity is realistic

The material which the students work with has been designed to look as authentic as possible. Most of the reading passages, for example, have been

1

written in ungraded English, so that the students have to scan, rather than read, to get the information they need from them.

This use of realistic materials is to help prepare the students for the ungraded, written English they will meet outside the classroom.

(see also Note on Scanning, section 4)

2   Using the activities in class

2.1   The format of the Student's Book

Each activity has been designed for pair work. The material is separated into two parts, one for each student in a pair, so that the two students have to ask each other for the information they need and come to a decision together.

The material for Student A is on a right hand page and the material for Student B is on the following left hand page. Student A material is marked with a single stripe in the top right hand corner of the page, and Student B material is marked with two stripes in the top left hand corner. Activities in which both students work with the same material have a broken stripe.

Instructions which outline the situation and the task(s) are given in the students' material.

2.2   Preparing for an activity

The teacher's notes for each activity provide a step-by-step guide on how to prepare the students. In each case, this preparation, or 'setting up' process runs along the following lines:

Familiarizing the students with the situation and the task(s)

Always give the students a few minutes to look through the material. Suggest that they read the instructions carefully, but only have a *brief* look at the rest of the material. It is important at this stage that they should grasp the general outline of the situation and the task(s) without getting involved in detail. Encourage them to ask you about points which they don't understand.

When they are ready, ask them the comprehension questions suggested in the teacher's notes for each activity under Setting Up.

(see also section 6.4)

Preparing and practising the language needed for the activity

A preparation stage, in which two students with the *same* material work together, has been built into each activity. During this stage, the students discuss the material together in detail and prepare the questions they will be asking their partners later. While they are doing this, you will be able to check that they are using the correct structures and lexis and help with any problems.

The specific tasks the students should do at this stage are outlined in the teacher's notes for each activity under Setting Up.

2.3   The activity itself

If the students have been fully prepared, they should have a clear idea of what to do and how to do it when they start working in pairs as Student A and Student B, so leave them to work independently of you.

Points which you may have to help the students with during the activity are given in the teacher's notes for each activity under Monitoring.

The Monitoring Check List (see section 6.5) outlines the points to watch for while the students are doing the activity.

2.4 Classroom organization

Seating

If possible, have the students in each pair sit opposite or at an angle to each other, so that they are not tempted to look at each other's material.

Try to ensure a reasonable distance between the pairs, so that they do not disturb each other's conversations.

Large classes

If there are a lot of students in your class it will be difficult to give each pair the time you need to monitor properly how well they are doing the activity. As a general rule, you should not try to monitor more than four or five separate conversations, so with a large class, have the students work in groups of four with two students working with the material for Student A and two students working with the material for Student B.

The third student

Not all classes have a conveniently even number of students, but if you can possibly help it, never work in a pair yourself with an extra 'odd' student. Always have the extra student work in a group of three, with the same material as one of the other students in the group.

Private lessons

There is no difficulty in adapting the activities if you only have one student. Work with one half of the material yourself while your student works with the other half. As far as possible, do the activity as a participant rather than as a teacher, and monitor your student without letting the notes which you take on his performance distract you too much from the conversation.

3 Fitting the activity into your teaching programme

3.1 Each activity is independent of the others

Each activity can be used independently of the others, and there is no reason why you should do them in the order in which they appear in the book. You can bring them into your programme as and when you feel they are necessary, taking into account the points outlined in section 3.2 below.

Whether you use a structural or functional approach will make very little difference, except that students who have been taught structurally may need more communicative practice while preparing for an activity, and students who have been taught functionally may need more structural consolidation.

3.2 How competent the students should be in the language needed for an activity before they attempt it

Even if the students have mastered the structures and lexis needed for an

3

activity in controlled situations such as drilling, lab exercises, dialogues, etc., there is no guarantee that they will be able to carry out the activity effectively.

They must be able to communicate with the structures and lexis as well. Essentially, this means that they must be used to asking questions which they don't already know the answers to, and then understanding, and perhaps commenting on, the answer they get.

For most students the gap between 'drilled' competence and sufficient communicative competence is not too difficult to bridge. The teacher's notes for each activity include several ideas for communicative exercises which use the activity's structures and lexis under the heading Preparation Activities. (see also section 6.3)

As a general rule, you should wait until the class are revising or consolidating a structure, and have perhaps done an exercise along the lines of those suggested in the Preparation Activities before you ask them to attempt the activity in their books.

3.3 Beginner or Intermediate? The minimum level for an activity

All of the activities can be done at a fairly low level, as long as the points outlined in section 3.2, above, are taken into account. The activities may occasionally look difficult, but with thorough preparation, as outlined under Setting Up in the teacher's notes for each activity, your students should have very few problems.

Activity 37, for example, looks forbidding because of the subject matter (politics and economy) and the long newspaper articles. However, it can be done well by lower-intermediate students if they have been properly introduced to scanning and have practised the necessary lexis and graph reading with the worksheet in their books (as described by the teacher's notes for the activity).

3.4 Using the activities at higher levels

The higher the level, the more the students can be encouraged to improvise around the basic conversation, adding comments and finding alternative ways of saying the same thing.

Once they have prepared for an activity (see section 2.2), you could ask them to use their material for occasional reference only while they're doing the activity, to increase their sense of spontaneity.

3.5 Progressive use of the activities

Getting used to a new approach

For most students, the activities in *Think Twice* will demand a way of working which they are unfamiliar with. They will probably need to have done two or three of the activities before they completely adjust and get the most out of them.

If your students have unusual difficulty in adjusting to the activities, get them to do activities 1, 2, and 3, in that order. This will give them a progressive introduction to the basic techniques used in the book.

Acquiring skills

Each activity in *Think Twice* gives the students practice in a number of skills, from scanning to organizing information to coping independently in English. These skills will only be mastered cumulatively, through regular use of the activities in *Think Twice* and similar materials.

4 Note on scanning

Scanning is the technique of looking quickly through a written passage to
find the information you want without reading the rest of it. The students
will have to use the technique in a large number of the activities in *Think Twice*.

4.1 *How to teach scanning*

Use the letter on page 9 of the Student's Book to get across the basic technique
of scanning:

Ask the students to look at the letter at the top of the page, and give them
a minute or so to look through it. (You might ask them to cover up the letter
at the bottom of the page so that they can't refer to it.) When they've finished,
ask them the questions next to the letter one by one. If the students don't
know the answer to a question, leave it and go on to the next one.

When you reach a point at which the students are unable to answer any
more of the questions, stop and tell them to look at the letter at the bottom
of the page. Then go through the questions again. This time the students
should be able to answer all the questions correctly.

At the end, ask them to find, and perhaps underline, the same information
in the letter at the top of the page.

Point out that the rest of the sentences are not important, and they don't
have to be able to understand them to get the basic information out of the
letter.

You could give the students further practice with another of the passages
in *Think Twice*, or a genuine letter or newspaper article. Get the students
to cover or turn the passage over so that they can't see it. Ask them a question
and give them fifteen seconds only to find the answer. At the end of the fifteen
seconds, stop them, tell them to cover or turn the passage over again, and
see who has found the answer. Then ask them another question which they
have fifteen seconds to find the answer to, and so on.

You could divide the class into two groups and have them race each other
to add a touch of urgency.

4.2 *The reading passages in the Student's Book*

Not all the passages are meant to be scanned. The teacher's notes for each
activity will tell you which are to be scanned and which aren't.

You could ask the students to translate the passages at home with a
dictionary, once they've done the activity, but only if you feel they could cope
and would profit from the exercise. A lot of idiomatic phrases and difficult
lexis have been put into the passages deliberately so that the students can't
understand them and are forced to scan. It would be pointless for most low-
level students to attempt to learn these.

4.3 *Student resistance to scanning*

If your students do not feel the usefulness or relevance of scanning, remind
them of material which they will automatically scan, such as railway
timetables, labels on tins, entertainment guides, etc.

You could also give them a newspaper or magazine in their native
language(s) and ask them to find the answer to a question about one of the
articles in it.

In each case, point out how irrelevant it is to read everything and how they should do exactly the same thing with authentic English timetables and magazines.

Stress that you want them to be able to function as efficiently as possible in English at the level they have already achieved instead of waiting until they are advanced students to be able to do so. The alternative would be to give them only graded material which they would find nowhere outside a classroom.

On the other hand, curiosity about what everything in a passage means is natural. To allow for this, you could either tell them that they can translate it at home after class, or promise that you will go through it, or read it out to them yourself in their native language(s) at the end of the activity.

(but see section 4.2 above)

5 The headings in the Teacher's Notes for each activity

5.1 Notes and Ideas

The notes for each activity are given under two main headings, 'Notes' and 'Ideas'.

The Notes deal with the activity itself, covering the Aim, Situation, Structures, Lexis, Setting Up, Monitoring, and Homework. The Ideas suggest other activities, discussions and improvisations which practise and extend the language used in the activity.

5.2 Aim   defines the structures or functions practised in the activity.

5.3 Situation   gives a general outline of the activity: the basic situation, what the students have to do and, in some cases, how they should do it.

It should be read in conjunction with the instructions for the activity in the Student's Book.

5.4 Structures   gives examples of the structures or functions practised in the activity, together with any other major structures which the students will need in order to carry out the activity.

Structures which the students will need in order to understand the instructions in their material have not been included, since the teacher can simply rephrase or explain these in class.

5.5 Lexis   gives the vocabulary the students will have to use during the activity.

Words which the majority of students will already know by the time they are capable of using the structures needed for the activity (i.e. at the level at which these structures are usually taught) have been left out. If you wish to find out *all* the lexis needed for a particular activity, do it yourself with another teacher, remembering that in most cases the letters or newspaper articles must be scanned, not read, and that the students should take the initiative of asking you about things they don't understand while they're preparing the activity.

(see also sections 4.2 and 6.1)

5.6   Setting Up   gives step by step instructions on how to introduce and prepare the students for the activity.

For most of the activities, these steps follow the same basic pattern (see section 2.2).

The teacher's questions in step 2 are only *suggested* questions and should be rephrased to suit the students' abilities. The suggested students' answers, in parentheses on the right, do not give the exact phrase with which the students should answer. They simply outline the information which each question is aiming at.

(see also section 6.4)

5.7   Monitoring   gives advice on the teacher's role while the students are doing the activity.

5.8   Solution   gives the correct answers to activities which have been designed along the lines of a puzzle.

This heading does not appear in the notes for every activity.

5.9   Homework   suggests a written piece of work which the students can do for homework. In each case, it recycles the structures and lexis used in the activity in a genuine written context (i.e. reports, letters, articles, etc.).

5.10   Preparation Activities   suggest various communicative activities which practise the structures used in the main activity. In most cases, the ideas can be adapted to bring in the lexis needed for the main activity as well.

The majority of these activities take very little preparation time. They should be treated as ideas to be adapted and extended according to the needs, abilities and level of your class. The range of suggested activities is intended to give the teacher a variety of ways to treat a particular structure in class (games, pair work, group work, etc.). They could be used after the students have done the main activity as well as before it. *Note:* Students will probably become bored with a structure if you have them do *all* of these activities.

5.11   Follow Up   suggests ways in which to relate the situation and language of the activity to the students' own experience. Usually, this is in the form of a class discussion.

(see also section 6.6)

5.12   Role-play (with video)   gives ideas for improvisations which recycle the language used in the activity. It also gives tips on how to set the scene and use the video camera effectively.

The majority of the ideas simply suggest ways of acting out the situation in the activity itself, so that the students are already familiar with the situation they are improvising.

This heading does not appear for every activity.

(see also section 6.7)

6 General Teaching Notes and Ideas

6.1 *Teaching the language needed for an activity*

The students must have the level of competence described in section 3.2 with the *structures* used in the activity. Don't try to pre-teach the structures just before they attempt an activity.

You can, however, pre-teach any lexis they need. For activities which require unusual lexis, the teacher's notes provide ideas on how to teach and practise it. Otherwise some general ideas for teaching lexis are as follows:

– Try to link the words together. This could be done by grouping them under general themes such as 'sport', 'transport', etc. For more disparate words, you could build them into a story or a dialogue. The story or dialogue could introduce the situation in the activity at the same time.
– Make the words memorable. Put them into sentences which create bizarre or striking pictures in the students' imaginations. Ask the students to exaggerate the pronunciation and say them very slowly or very quickly.
– Only teach seven to ten words at a time.

Before you plan how to pre-teach the lexis, consider whether or not you need to pre-teach it at all. The students will come across most of the lexis they will need while they are preparing for the activity, and should be encouraged to take the initiative themselves to ask you what the words mean. If, during the activity, they have to find a way of explaining them to their partner, that in itself is a useful exercise.

6.2 *Note-taking*

In many of the activities, the students will have to take notes to keep track of the information. They should be discouraged from writing everything down in complete sentences, as this will slow them down and reduce the spontaneity of their conversation.

For most students, firm and constant reminders to take notes, and not write sentences, should be enough. Other students may need to learn and practise the skill with simple exercises like the following:

Write out one or two sentences on the board in full, and tell the students to write them again in note form. Then ask the class which words in the sentences are the important ones. Once they've isolated the important words, ask them to check whether their notes only contain these words, or whether they include any unnecessary language. Write up a few new sentences for the students to practise with.

After that you could write sentences in note form on the board, and have the students work out what the complete sentences are.

Finally, to point out the usefulness of taking notes, read them a passage too quickly for them to write everything out, and ask them to summarize it from their notes. This can be done with very low levels. For example, the passage you read could simply be about three people, where each one lives, and what each one has got. It should produce notes along the lines of 'John lives – Berlin, has got – 2 dogs. Mary ...'

6.3 *Simple communicative exercises*

The activities in *Think Twice* and the preparation activities which accompany them are designed to come after a structure has been introduced, drilled, practised, etc. However, it is possible to have the students work communicatively at a much earlier stage with simple exercises you can create yourself.

The basic element of a communicative exercise is simply that one student has the questions and another student has the answers. The following example is to practise the Simple Past and the Simple Present. The students work in pairs (A and B):

A

THE STORY OF ALEX

	Usually	Yesterday	Why
get up (when):			
go to work (how):			
start work (when):			
have lunch (where):			

THE STORY OF SUE

	Usually	Yesterday	Why
get up (when):	8.30	7.30	She wanted to take her car to the garage.
go to work (how):	car	bus	She didn't have her car.
start work (when):	9.30	9.00	She arrived early.
have lunch (where):	canteen	restaurant	A client invited her to lunch.

B

THE STORY OF ALEX

	Usually	Yesterday	Why
get up (when):	7.30	9.00	His alarm clock didn't work.
go to work (how):	bus	taxi	He was late.
start work (when):	9.00	10.00	He arrived at 9.55.
have lunch (where):	restaurant	at work	He didn't have enough time to leave the office.

THE STORY OF SUE

	Usually	Yesterday	Why
get up (when):			
go to work (how):			
start work (when):			
have lunch (where):			

Before they start the exercise, tell them to ask a question only if they don't already know the answer, and to note the answer they get. Also run through the basic question and answer pattern with them to make sure they understand what to do. (In this example, the question pattern is: 'When does (Alex) usually get up?' 'When did (he) get up yesterday?' 'Why did he get up at nine o'clock?'.)

With your own exercises, make sure that they are presented clearly. The students must be able to understand what they should be asking or answering, and be able to go from one question to the next without asking you for help. As with the main activities in *Think Twice*, your students will probably have to do two or three of these exercises before they get used to them.

6.4 Setting-up alternatives

The suggested setting-up process can be adapted in a number of ways, depending on your particular style of teaching and the needs of your class.

The situation can be presented through drawings, a story, a dialogue, or, if you have access to it, the video improvisation which another class has done for that activity (see section 6.7).

While you're discussing the situation with the students, you could help them to imagine it more clearly by asking questions which relate it to their experience. If the activity is about noisy neighbours (Activity 17) ask them if they have noisy neighbours; if it's set in Rome (Activity 33) ask them if they've been to Rome, and so on.

During the stage at which students with the same material work together to prepare and practise the language they will need for the activity, the students could work in groups rather than pairs.

6.5 Monitoring

Intervening

Although generally you should not intervene while the students are doing an activity, there are two cases in which you could usefully do so.

The first is if the students resort to their native language. Every time they do one of the activities, insist that they say *everything* in English. You could pre-teach them phrases such as 'I don't understand', 'What's next?', 'Just a minute', etc. to help them with this. An alternative which works very effectively is to note what they say in their native language(s) during an activity and work out the translations with them afterwards.

The second case is if the students have problems organizing their material. In activities where this could prove difficult, the teacher's notes will give you ideas for how to advise your students.

In general, if you do intervene, intervene as a (temporary) participant rather than as a teacher.

Monitoring Check List

While the students are carrying out an activity, watch for the following points:
– Do they get information across quickly and clearly?
– Are they accurate?
– If they take 'short cuts' (single words, etc.) are these effective and natural?
– Do they introduce extra language to vary the conversation, and if so, how well?
– How well do they improvise language they haven't been taught?

Try to get an idea of a student's general performance, noting at least one strong point and one weak point for each student.

Always have a brief discussion with the students at the end of an activity to bring out these points and generally correct mistakes. If possible, get them to comment on their own performance.

6.6 Leading follow-up discussions with low-level students

During a discussion of the kind suggested in the Follow Up for each activity, you may find the following ideas useful.

Keep the pattern of questions you ask more or less the same for each student, so that they can anticipate what is coming, but also put in the occasional 'surprise' question.

Limit your conversation with each student to two or three questions to maintain the pace and class interest.

As soon as possible, get other students to take over the conversation and ask the questions.

If the conversation proves slow and difficult, stop it and give the students a few minutes to note down ideas before you start again.

6.7 Video

The improvisation
Keep the improvisations short. Three or four minutes should be enough to bring out the main points, and hold the students' interest when you're playing the tape back.

Have the technical side prepared in advance so that you can start filming with as little fuss as possible.

Students are often shy about acting in front of a camera. Usually the best way to help them to overcome this is to get them used to it with simple, regular improvisations in class. For example, you could start with a student simply sitting behind his desk and talking about a subject of his choice to the camera. You can then build progressively through conversations and discussions before you ask them to get up and act.

Adapting the improvisations for a tape recorder
Most of the video ideas for the activities suggest how to set the scene and bring out what is happening *visually*. With a tape recorder, the same thing can be done with sound effects.

While you are preparing for an improvisation, imagine what you would need to know if you didn't know anything at all about the situation. If someone opens a door, or answers a phone, the people who listen to the tape must hear a door opening or a phone ringing.

There is no need to have the actual sound effects. The students who are not in the improvisation could be asked to make them themselves with their voices, bangs on the table, etc.

As with video, the improvisation should last no longer than three or four minutes.

Using video improvisations to set up an activity
If one of your classes has done the video improvisation suggested for an activity, you could use the recording to introduce the activity to a different class.

Alternatively, you could do the improvisations yourself with other teachers. Substitute the information in the students' material with new information (e.g. if a train leaves at 6.30 in one of the activities, it could leave at 8.15 during the improvisation) so that you can use the recording either to introduce the activity or as a listening comprehension after the activity.

6.8 *Using the activities with mixed-level classes*

There are several ways of adapting the activities if some students in your class are much stronger than others.

You could get strong students to work together and weak students to work together. While the students are preparing for the activity, devote most of your time to helping the weak students, and allow the strong students to start the activity whenever they are ready.

Inevitably, the strong students will finish earlier than the others. You could ask them to do the activity again, perhaps exchanging roles, or without looking at their material (tell them to improvise details they've forgotten). Alternatively, if your video equipment is set up in a different room and your students can operate it, you could leave them to prepare and record the improvisation.

If you decide to put a strong student and a weak student together, this can be useful during the preparation stage (see section 2.2) but generally avoid unequal partnerships during the activity itself. Even if a strong student is naturally patient and helpful, he'll be robbed of much of the challenge of the activity if he's paired with a weak student.

7   If the activity goes badly: Check List

1. Were the students sufficiently prepared linguistically? (see sections 2.2, 3.2 and 6.1)
2. Were they sufficiently trained in the skills they had to use? (see sections 4 and 6.2)
3. Is this the first time your students have done an activity like this? (see sections 3.5 and 6.3)
4. Did they fully understand the situation? (see sections 2.2 and 6.4)
5. Did they rush the preparation period? (see sections 2.2 and 6.4)

8   Abbreviations, etc. used in the Student's and Teacher's Books

Student A and Student B are frequently referred to as St.A and St.B respectively.

The teacher is usually addressed directly as 'you' in the teacher's notes.

The pronouns used for 'a student', 'your partner', etc. are 'he' or 'him', rather than 'she' or 'her'. This is common practice in English, and thus the form students are most likely to come across elsewhere.

The lexis used in the Role-play (with video) section of the notes for each activity is as follows:

pan:	rotate the camera from side to side
tilt:	tip the camera upwards or downwards
zoom in:	move from a general picture to a close-up
zoom out:	move from a close-up to a general picture

Notes and Ideas for the activities

1 MISSING!

Notes

AIM To practise talking about personal identity with *to be*; the use of the alphabet and numbers.

SITUATION A man has disappeared. His clothes have been found on the beach. The police (the students) would like to know who he is.

   The students work in pairs. Student A (St.A) has the driving licence, library card, etc. which have been taken from the man's pockets. Student B (St.B) has the police Missing Persons Declaration Form. St.B asks St.A for the information he needs to fill in the form.

STRUCTURES *What's his (surname)?*
Is he married?
Can you spell that please?

LEXIS

surname	*telephone number*	*married*	numbers 1–10
first name	*job*		the alphabet
address	*avenue*	*Mr/Mrs/Miss/Ms*	

Note: Students should be left to cope with the rest of the lexis (marital status, date of birth, occupation) if you feel they can make an intelligent guess at what each one means.

SETTING UP
1. Ask half the class to look at the material for Student A and half the class to look at the material for Student B.
2. Get the students to look at the pictures at the top of their material. Ask:

Picture 1:	Where's this man?	(on the beach)
Picture 2:	Where is he now?	(in the water)
	What's on the beach?	(his clothes)
Picture 3:	Where is he now?	(I don't know)
Picture 4:	Who is this man?	(a policeman)
Picture 5:	Where's the policeman now?	(at the police station)
	What's on the table?	(the clothes)
	What's in the pockets?	(St.A: The man's passport, etc.)

3. You could let the students look briefly at each other's material, so that they're sure about what they have to do.
   You could also ask a student to empty his pockets of cheque book, identity card, etc. and have two different students act the parts of police officers finding out about him.
4. Bring the two halves of the class together in pairs and leave them to it.

MONITORING If a student with St.A material is having problems finding the answers, his partner could help him to look for them – but *only* if St.A *asks* for him to do so. You could pre-teach 'Please help!' or 'Can you help me?' for this. Don't intervene. Students should cope for themselves. Instead, watch for how well they communicate (see Introduction, section 6.5).

SOLUTION   *Surname:* Sutcliff   *First names:* Stephen Paul
⟨Mr⟩/Mrs/Miss/Ms   *Marital status:* married   *Date of birth:* 31/08/50
Address: 5 Longford Avenue, Ryeport   *Tel:* 683672
Occupation: Finance officer

HOMEWORK   Students could fill in a Declaration Form with details about themselves. In the following class they could exchange their forms and repeat the activity, but to find out about each other this time.

Ideas

PREPARATION
ACTIVITIES

What's your/his (name)?

Forms   There are all sorts of forms the students can fill in for names, addresses, etc., with one student acting the part of the receptionist or clerk, and the other student acting the part of the customer. Simply explain the situation and draw a sample form on the board for the students to copy.

You could introduce one or two new phrases, depending on the type of form you use, e.g. 'Can I have a room?' (hotel), 'What's my teacher's name?' (registering for English classes), 'Please send two bottles of champagne' (ordering over the phone), 'What's your company's address?' (filling in an income tax form).

Car accident   Bring in a picture of a car accident. Tell two students they are the drivers of the cars and have them mime getting out of the cars and asking each other for their names, addresses, etc. and the name of their insurance companies.

You could complicate the situation by introducing 'It's not my car!' so the students have to ask for details about both the driver and the owner of the car.

Telegrams   Prepare a set of cards with 'The telegram is to . . .' and 'The message is . . .' on each card. Write in names and messages which revise language you've taught, or get the students to invent them.

Students work in pairs. One wants to send a telegram and has one of the cards. The other is the telegram clerk (in a Post Office) or operator (over the phone). Run through the clerk's questions with the students before they start.

If possible, give the students real telegram forms to use (not necessarily in English).

FOLLOW UP   Get each student to leave an article of clothing or object on a table in the front of the room together with an identity card, cheque book, or library card, etc.

One student could then be the assistant in a lost property office while another student comes to claim something ('That's my coat!'). The assistant should be naturally suspicious and refuse to give up the object until the person who's lost it has given his address, phone number, etc. correctly.

14

1: Missing!

A passenger loses his wallet on a bus. Two bus conductors find it, and note the owner's name, address and phone number.

Arrange half a dozen chairs to suggest seats in a bus. Place the camera so that all the seats are facing it. The video starts with a student sitting in one of the 'front' seats with his coat next to him, covering his wallet. The student gets up, takes his coat and leaves. Zoom in on the wallet left on the seat. Then zoom out again and tilt the camera – keeping the wallet in the bottom of the image – to take in the two conductors coming up the 'aisle' of the bus. Keep the same image while the conductors find the wallet and discuss its owner.

2 THE SOCIAL SECURITY

Notes

AIM
To practise talking about personal identity with *to be;* the use of the alphabet and numbers.

SITUATION
Two secretaries (the students) at the Social Security offices have to transfer the information about four people from individual forms to a file card.

Each student has the individual forms for two people and a file card with the four surnames. Each fills in as much of his file card as he can and then asks his partner about the other people.

STRUCTURES
What's | *his*
___ | *Miss Rawling's* | *first name?*

Is she married?
Can you spell that please?

LEXIS
surname	*telephone number*	*children*	*married*	the alphabet
first name	*wife*	*road*	*single*	numbers 1–10
address	*mother*	*street*	*divorced*	

Note: You could teach *Has she got any (children)?*, or leave the student to invent something along the lines of 'Dependants?' 'Yes, two children.' Students should be able to deduce the meaning of *marital status, dependants, social security number* and *none* by themselves.

SETTING UP
1. Ask half the class to look at the material for Student A and half the class to look at the material for Student B.
2. If you wish, get the students to look at the instructions, and ask:
   What's your job?　(a secretary)
   Where?　　　　　(at the Social Security offices)
   You might also discuss what a form is, where you use one, and what information is needed for these ones.
   If no comparable system to the Social Security exists in the students' country, simply explain that it gives you money if you're unemployed.
3. Ask the students with the *same* material to work in pairs. One student looks at the large file card and asks the questions while the other student looks at the small, individual cards and gives the answers. When they've finished filling in the details for one person, they exchange roles.
   Use this period to check that they are using the correct language and · help with problems.
4. Bring the two halves of the class together in pairs, and leave them to it.

MONITORING
Don't intervene. Students should cope for themselves. Instead, watch for how well they communicate (see Introduction, section 6.5).

HOMEWORK   The students could write a simple letter about themselves to the Social Security containing the information on the forms and anything else they feel is necessary (e.g. nationality, age, etc.).

Ideas

PREPARATION
ACTIVITIES

What's (Mr Rolston's) address?

See the ideas for Activity 1.

Group and pair work   Divide the class into two halves. In each half, everyone asks everyone else for their names, addresses, if they're married, etc., and notes the answers.

When they've finished, bring the two halves of the class together in pairs. Each student can then ask his partner about the rest of the people in the class ('What's André's surname?').

You could then ask them to check their information with the students themselves ('André, is your surname Casavates?').

Guessing   Give each student two blank cards, or slips of paper. Tell them to write their addresses on one card, and their phone numbers on the other. They should then write their names on the back of both cards. When they've finished, collect the cards together.

Divide the class into two or four groups, depending on the size of the class. Spread half (or a quarter) of the cards out on a desk in the middle of each group. Keep the name side of each card down, so that students can only see the addresses or phone numbers.

The students try to guess whose addresses or phone numbers are on the cards ('Is that Marie's address?'). Someone could check the name side of the card and answer ('No, it's John's address.').

You could also introduce *I think,* e.g. 'I think that's Marie's address.'

FOLLOW UP   Students could rearrange the class as a Social Security office with reception desks. Some students take on the roles of clerks and sit at the desks, while the others line up to apply for social security. The clerks should fill in forms for the applicants like the ones in the activity.

ROLE-PLAY
(WITH VIDEO)

Have the students do the Follow Up idea as a video improvisation.

Position the camera behind the reception desk and the clerk. For each applicant, start with an image which takes in the applicant, the desk, and a back view of the social security clerk. Zoom in on the form while the clerk is filling it in. At the end, zoom out again to the original image.

3 BUSINESS CARDS

Notes

AIM   To practise talking about personal identity with *to be* and/or the Simple Present; the use of the alphabet and numbers.

SITUATION   The students have met a number of people at a business reception. Some of these people have given them their business cards, others have not.

    Each student has three business cards. He also has a list of other people he's met, but hasn't got the business cards for. He asks his partner about them.

Note: Neither student has the business cards for *all* the people on his partner's list, and in some cases a person's job is given on the list rather than his or her name. The students should be left to cope with these points as they come across them.

STRUCTURES   What's | his | first name?
                  | Mr Paquès' |

What's his job?   or   What does he do?
What's her company? or Where does she work?
Can you spell that please?

LEXIS
manager	sales representative	phone number
accountant	first name	reception
(managing) editor	address	card
sales manager		

SETTING UP   1. Ask half the class to look at the material for Student A and half the class to look at the material for Student B.

2. Get the students to look at the picture at the top of their material. Ask:

Where is this?	(a reception)
Who's at the reception?	(Dan Smith, Corinne Mills, Judith Bitting and Dag Rudvin)
What's Mr Rudvin's address?	(Students answer with the business card)
job? etc.	
What's Dan Smith's job?	(I don't know)
Why not?	(I haven't got his card)
Have you got Corinne Mills' card?	(St.A: No, I haven't)
	(St.B: Yes, I have)
Have you got Judith Bitting's card?	(St.A: Yes, I have)
	(St.B: No, I haven't)

Select two students, one from each half of the class, to demonstrate the task by asking each other one or two questions about Judith and Corinne.

3. Give the students a few minutes to look through the rest of their cards and the list. Encourage them to ask you about anything they don't understand.

    If you like, you could have students with the *same* material work in pairs to practise asking and answering questions about the people they've got cards for.

4. Bring the two halves of the class together in pairs and leave them to it.

Don't intervene. Students should cope for themselves. Instead, watch for how well they communicate (see Introduction, section 6.5).

HOMEWORK Students design their own business or personal cards.

Ideas

PREPARATION ACTIVITIES

What do you/does he (do)?

Group and pair work   Adapt the 'group and pair work' idea for Activity 2 by changing the questions ('What do you do?' 'Where do you live/work/come from?').

Assembling business cards   Write out four names, four addresses, four jobs, four company names, and four telephone numbers. Each of these should be on a small, separate piece of paper, so there are twenty pieces in all. Put all the pieces into an envelope. Prepare as many envelopes as you have students. Each envelope should contain the *same* names, the *same* addresses, etc. (The easiest way to prepare this is to write everything on one sheet of paper, make as many photocopies as you need, and then cut them up.)

   Put the students into pairs and give one envelope to each student. One student assembles a business card without his partner seeing it. His partner then has to assemble the same card from the pieces in his own envelope by asking questions. When they've finished, they check that their cards are the same, mix the pieces up and start again.

   The activity could also be used to practise 'Does (Anne) work for (Philips)?', '... live in (London)?', etc.

Getting home   (This activity also practises directions, prepositions, and *first, second,* etc.) Bring in a map of the area around your school. Tell the students that everyone's car has broken down except yours – and you will take them all home after the class. They must use the map to plan the best route and explain it to you ('Take Andrea home first. She lives in the south, here. Then ...').

   When they've got the idea, divide the class into groups. Appoint one person in each group to pick the others up from work and then take them home. 'What time do you finish work?' could help to complicate matters.

FOLLOW UP   – Ask the students to prepare a diagram of the hierarchy of the company they work in and explain it to the others. If they only put people's names in the diagram (leaving out the jobs), the other students could ask 'What does ... do?'
   – Students ask each other 'Do you know a good doctor? lawyer? plumber? etc.' and give genuine answers (name, address, etc.).

ROLE-PLAY (WITH VIDEO)   Have the students improvise the situation in the activity with real business cards.
   Put two students at either end of a small table. Both should be facing the camera, and, if possible, have a toy telephone on the table next to them.
   Keep both students in the image while one dials the other's number, says hello, etc. Zoom in on the business card when the second student starts talking about it (You'll have to warn him to hold the card at an angle so that both he and the camera can see it.)

4 HOLIDAY PHOTOS

Notes

AIM To practise talking about family relations with *to be*.

SITUATION The students show each other holiday photos and discuss the people in them (their names, how they're related to each other and where they are).

The material for each student includes two photos and part of a letter giving information about his partner's photos. In turn, each student shows his photos to his partner, so he can point to the people he wants to ask about, and his partner finds the answers in his letter.

The students then fill in their respective family trees with the correct names. (*Note:* each student has one 'odd' person who will not fit into the tree.)

STRUCTURES *Who's that?*
Is she (Karen's) mother?
Where are they?
What's his name?
Can you spell that?

LEXIS
mother	brother	son	husband	on the left
father	sister	daughter	wife	on the right
			friend	

SETTING UP 1. Ask half the class to look at the material for student A, and half the class to look at the material for student B.
2. Ask:
Is (Karen/Aziz) at home?	(No. On holiday)
What are these?	(her/his photos)
Who's in the photos?	(I don't know)
Who's your letter from?	(St.A: Karen)
	(St.B: Aziz)
Is it about *your* photos or your partner's?	(my partner's)
3. Put the students with the *same* material together in pairs. Tell them to prepare the questions to ask about their photos and to read the letter carefully.
4. When they're ready, bring the two halves of the class together in pairs. Point out that they should, in turn, show each other their photos and ask about them.
   Remind them to fill in the family tree. Then leave them to it.

MONITORING Since the students are looking at each other's material, some students may start reading their partner's letter. You could anticipate this by asking students who are showing their photos to cover up the letter at the bottom with a piece of paper.

Otherwise don't intervene. Students should cope for themselves. Instead, watch for how well they communicate (see Introduction, section 6.5).

HOMEWORK Students enclose their own holiday snaps in a letter to a friend, explaining who's who and where they are.

Ideas

Family relations

Family trees   Draw a large family tree on a piece of paper, with space for
pictures, like this:

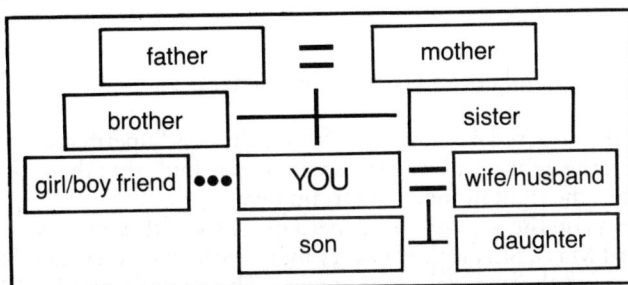

father	=	mother
brother		sister
girl/boy friend •••	YOU =	wife/husband
son		daughter

Note: label
the box in the
middle 'you',
but don't label
any of the
other boxes.

Cut out pictures from magazines, or have the students bring in photos of
their own families. One student then holds up a picture or photo and the
others ask him 'Who's that?' or 'Is that your (mother)?' He answers 'This
is my (wife).' and places it in the correct position on the family tree. The
other students could then ask 'What's her name?' and/or 'How old is she?',
etc.
   With more family trees and pictures, the class could work in small groups.
   If you put a picture of 'John' or 'Susan' in the 'you' box, the students
can practise '*his* mother', '*her* father', etc.

Russian novels   Bring in a novel with the kind of character list which shows
how each character is related to each other (or write such a list yourself)
and have the students draw up a family tree.
   Soap operas which the students know, like *Dallas*, work well for this.
   If you bring in the lists for two different novels, and have half the students
do each, they can explain their family trees to each other afterwards.

Adapt the Homework suggestion by having the students discuss their family
snaps with each other. They will be better prepared for this if they've already
written the letter suggested in Homework and have had a chance to look
up the vocabulary they need.

Video the Follow Up suggestion. If you have the two students stand or sit
next to each other, and hold the snapshots or photo album so that both they
and the camera can see them, you will be able to vary the camera work by
zooming in on the photographs from time to time.

5 THE DELIVERY MAN

Notes

AIM To practise using numbers and correcting mistakes.

SITUATION Mrs Barnes has ordered her shopping from Saleways Supermarket over the phone. When the delivery man arrives with it, she finds that the supermarket hasn't sent her the right number of certain items.

The students do the activity *twice*, perhaps in two different lessons. The first time (3rd May), St.A is the delivery man (with an invoice) and St.B is Mrs Barnes (with the original shopping list). The second time (10th May), the roles are reversed.

The first list and invoice deal with numbers between one and twenty. The second list and invoice compare *-teen* and *-ty* e.g. 17 and 70. Both lists have the same food items on them.

STRUCTURES Delivery Man: *Four packets of cornflakes.*
Mrs Barnes: *Yes, that's right.*
DM: *Five tins of tuna.*
Mrs B: *No, three tins of tuna.*
DM: *Three tins?*
Mrs B: *Yes.*
DM: (changing his invoice) *Sorry. Three tins.*

LEXIS *packet*   *large*   *That's right.*
tin   *small*   *Sorry.*
delivery man *medium*

SETTING UP 1. Ask half the class to look at the material for Student A and half the class to look at the material for Student B.
2. Get all the students to look at the tins and packets of food at the top of their page, and work out what's what from their invoice or list.
3. When they have matched the food in the picture with the food in the invoice or list, ask:

Top picture: Who's the woman? (Mrs Barnes)
Where is she?   (at home)
Who's the man?   (the delivery man)
Where is he?   (in a shop)

You could have two students improvise the phone conversation at this point, along the lines of: 'Good morning. Saleways Supermarket.' 'Good morning. This is Mrs Barnes. (Can I have) three tins of tuna, please?'. Then ask:

Bottom picture: Where's the delivery man? (at Mrs Barnes' house)
Is Mrs Barnes happy?   (no)
Why not?   (three tins, not five tins)

Again, you could have the students improvise the conversation (see Structures). Encourage them to mime taking the things out of the box and putting them on the table.

22

4. Bring the class together in pairs. Tell them to look at list or invoice number 1, and ask 'Who are you?' (St.A: the delivery man, St.B: Mrs Barnes).
   Point out that the delivery man should correct his invoice whenever there is a mistake on it, and then leave them to it.

MONITORING   When they've finished number 1, the delivery man should compare his corrected invoice with his partner's shopping list. Each pair then goes on to number 2 (or you could reserve this for the following lesson).
   Don't intervene. Students should cope for themselves. Instead, watch for how well they communicate (see Introduction, section 6.5).

Ideas

PREPARATION
ACTIVITIES

Numbers and letters

Bingo   Dictate ten to fifteen numbers which the students are having problems with. Tell the students to circle three of them. When they're ready, call out numbers from the list at random. As soon as a student has heard all three of his circled numbers called, he shouts 'Bingo!' (and wins). Repeat the activity with the students calling out the numbers.

Codes   Invent codes by assigning numbers to letters. Use numbers which the students have problems with. Then, in pairs, give one student a message in code and the other the key to the code (e.g. St.A: 'What's 17?' St.B: 'It's E.').
   Students could also encode their own messages (St.A: 'What's A?' St.B: 'It's 12.') to pass to other people in the class, and/or invent their own codes.

Correcting mistakes

Telephone numbers   In pairs, give one student a list of, say, five telephone numbers, and the other student a list of five numbers which are the same except for one or two figures. They then have five mini conversations like this: 'Hello, is that 841 90 06?' 'No, this is 841 80 06.' 'Oh. Sorry.'

FOLLOW UP   Create your own lists and invoices, perhaps having the supermarket deliver the wrong packet size, or the wrong brand for some items. You could also change the context, e.g. ordering lunch from a takeaway, or drinks from an off-licence.

ROLE-PLAY
(WITH VIDEO)   The students rearrange the classroom as a restaurant. Some students are the waiters, the rest are customers. The customers give their orders, and the waiters bring back the wrong things. Introduce something like '*Excuse me, but* it's two hamburgers and a pizza, not three hamburgers' to make the customers' complaints more polite.
   Video one pair or group of customers at a time, and remind the other students to keep their conversation subdued until it's their turn. When you've finished with one 'table', simply press the pause button on the camera and move it to the next 'table' before continuing. Keep the camera close to each table so that the other customers in the background are slightly out of focus.

6 HOLIDAY HOTELS

Notes

AIM To practise the use of *it is* and *there is*.

SITUATION John (St.A) is on holiday at the Piano Hotel in Corsica. Carol (St.B) is also on holiday in Corsica, but she's staying at the Marina Hotel. Neither John nor Carol are entirely happy with their hotels, and they'd like to find different ones. The students have to find out whether Carol's hotel would suit John and vice versa.

St.A has a short description of the Piano Hotel and a postcard from John explaining what he likes and doesn't like about it. St.B has the same for Carol and the Marina Hotel.

STRUCTURES *Is there (a discotheque)?*
Is it (noisy)?

LEXIS *to want*   *tennis court*   *lovely*
to stay   *beach*   *crowded*
market   *cheap*
shop   *expensive*
postcard   *noisy*
brochure

SETTING UP 1. Ask half the class to look at the material for Student A and half the class to look at the material for Student B.
2. Ask St.A students:
   Where is John?   (he's in Corsica)
   What's the name of his hotel?   (the Piano Hotel)
   What's the town near the hotel?   (Valettio)
   Ask St.B students the same questions for Carol.
3. Have students with the *same* material work in pairs, to familiarize themselves with what the hotel and the town have to offer. One way of doing this is to write a list on the board of the amenities one usually finds in a hotel or holiday town (restaurants, swimming pool, etc.). One student can then use the prompts on the board to ask questions ('Is there . . .?') while the other looks for answers.
   When they've finished, ask them to read the postcard and write two lists – one list of what John (or Carol) thinks is good about the holiday, and one of what he (or she) thinks isn't good. Tell them not to worry about phrases which they don't understand. Use this period to check that the students are using the structures and lexis correctly, and help with any problems.
4. Ask the class as a whole:
   What's a perfect hotel for John (Carol)?   (students describe such a hotel using their 'good/not good' lists)
   What does John (Carol) want to do?   (stay at a different hotel)
   Bring the two halves of the class together in pairs and tell them to find out if Carol's hotel is right for John and vice versa.

24

MONITORING If you like, encourage the students to role-play the situation over the telephone or over a meal in the hotel restaurant. Otherwise, don't intervene. Leave them to cope for themselves and watch for how well they communicate (see Introduction, section 6.5). At the end of the activity, ask the students to justify their conclusions.

SOLUTION   The Piano Hotel might suit Carol, although she would miss the village market, but the Marina Hotel probably wouldn't suit John because it and the beach are very crowded.

HOMEWORK   Students write a letter to a friend describing the area around their homes, and explaining why they are – or are not – happy with it.

Ideas

There is/it is

PREPARATION ACTIVITIES   Adapt the *What's it like?* ideas for Activity 14 to include *there is/are*. As in the ideas below, the simplest way of doing this would be to write a list of *possible* amenities or objects on the board, so the students have to ask 'Is there...?' before they can ask 'What's it like?'

Where are you?   Write the names of four or five villages (imaginary) on the board, and, using the students' ideas, list under the names what there is or isn't in each village.

In pairs or small groups, one student imagines he's in one of the villages. His partner(s) then asks him 'Is there a...?' until they can guess which village the student is thinking about ('You're in...'). To bring in the contrast with *Is it...?*, simply add an adjective in brackets after each amenity on the board.

For homework, students write a postcard about one of the villages without giving its name. In the next class, each student gives his postcard to another student who then has to guess which village he has written about.

Hotels   On the board, write a general list of the amenities you could find in a hotel with various adjectives to describe them (e.g. shop – large/cheap/crowded, etc.). Divide the class into two halves and tell each half to imagine they're staying at a hotel. Ask them to decide what amenities there are in their hotel, and what they are like.

When they've finished, bring the class together in pairs, and ask each student to find out about his partner's hotel. You could set the scene that they are both on holiday, staying at different hotels, and they meet on the beach or in a café.

FOLLOW UP   Students describe advertisements they like or dislike.

They could also ask each other about the area around their homes, as in the Homework idea, e.g. 'Is there a bank near your house?' 'Yes, there is.' 'Is it Barclays or Lloyds?'

ROLE-PLAY (WITH VIDEO)   A student comes into a travel agency to enquire about different hotels.

The student playing the travel agent sits behind a table and has a brochure with hotels in it. The student playing the tourist sits in front of the table.

Keep the camera a little behind and to one side of the student playing the tourist so you can zoom in over his shoulder to show the hotels in the brochure which the travel agent is talking about.

7 ADVERTISEMENTS

Notes

AIM
To practise using simple adjectives to describe people; *too* and *enough*.

SITUATION
An advertising agency (St.B) is looking for a face to market a product, so it consults a model agency (St.A).

St.B has two advertisements, one for soap and the other for tea. He decides what kind of model (or models) he needs for each (i.e. man or woman, young or old, etc.), and then explains this to St.A. St.A has photographs of a variety of models whom he can suggest.

STRUCTURES
What do you think of (him)?
She's too young.
Is she old enough?

LEXIS
to look (for)	*advertisement*	*young*	*gentle*	*beautiful*
	model	*old*	*romantic*	*friendly*
	soap	*thin* (slim)	*ugly*	
	tea	*fat* (chubby)	*sexy*	*very*
		hard		

SETTING UP
1. Ask half the class to look at the material for Student A and half the class to look at the material for Student B.
2. Ask St.A students:
   What are these?   (photographs of models)
   Then get them to discuss the models together. Ask them to find as many adjectives as they can to describe them, or put the Lexis adjectives on the board, and ask them to choose which adjectives they think are most suitable for which models.
3. Ask St.B students:
   What are these?   (advertisements)
   What are you looking for?   (models for them)
   Then get them to discuss together what kind of models they're looking for for each advertisement, whether the model should be a man or a woman, romantic or sexy, etc. Each student should be encouraged to have his own opinion.
   Go around both groups helping with vocabulary and ideas.
4. When both groups have finished, bring them together in pairs. Point out that the St.B students want models and the St.A students have got models.
   You may want to have one pair improvise the first part of the conversation in front of the class, e.g.:
   St.B: Good morning. I'm looking for a model.
   St.A: Yes sir. A man or a woman?
   St.B: I'm looking for . . .
   St.A: Fine. What do you think of (him)? (St.A shows St.B the model he is referring to)
   etc. (see Structures)
   When you're sure they've all understood, leave them to it.

MONITORING Don't intervene. Students should cope for themselves. Instead, watch for how well they communicate (see Introduction, section 6.5).

HOMEWORK Students could write a postcard to a friend describing the people in their English school ('My teacher is . . ., the receptionist is . . .,' etc.) or at a holiday camp ('The tennis instructor is . . ., my new girl-friend is . . .') or at any other place they can think of.

Ideas

PREPARATION
ACTIVITIES

Descriptions of people, too and enough

Drawing Choose a student and attempt to draw him or her on the board. Don't take too long over it, don't try to make a good job of it, and tell the class who you're drawing so they don't have to guess!

Get the students to criticize the sketch as you're drawing it, e.g. the eyes are too big, the nose isn't thin enough, she isn't sexy enough, etc. Then get them to draw each other and criticize each other's drawings in the process.

Nationalities Bring in a collection of magazine photos of people and have the students argue over where each person comes from. You might introduce the phrase *She looks . . .*, e.g. 'I think she looks French.' 'Why?' 'Because she's got dark eyes and a long face.', etc.

Hotel rooms (sketch) Two students are tourists and a third is a hotel receptionist showing them the rooms available in the hotel. The tourists admit some good points in each room ('it's very large', 'it's quiet enough', etc.) but also point out its faults ('it's too noisy'). They go on until they find a room which satisfies them.

You might make a set of prompt cards to help them, e.g. 'Room 101: light enough but too noisy. Bed very hard.'

ROLE-PLAY
(WITH VIDEO)

Shopping. One student is a customer, another is a shop assistant. The customer tries on different coats until he finds one he likes. The conversation follows the same lines as in the activity, but with adjectives like *long/short/expensive/large/small/heavy*.

The 'shop' can be simply set up by having all the students put their coats or jackets on a table pushed against one wall of the classroom. If your students enjoy acting you could also ask them to imagine that there is a long mirror a little to the right or left of the camera.

Keep the camera fairly static throughout the improvisation, unless you really feel certain moments should be highlighted by zooming closer in.

8 EXCHANGES

Notes

AIM   To practise *have got* and *to want*.

SITUATION   Swop Shop is a (fictional) agency in London which organizes exchanges of household objects between people. Anyone wanting to exchange fills in a form describing what he has got and the things he would like to exchange it for.

Each student has seven of these forms. Together they have to find out which people can exchange.

STRUCTURES   *Has anyone got (a double bed)?* or *Who's got (a double bed)?*
Does she want (a washing machine)?

LEXIS

table	bookcase	black and white	telephone numbers
chair	mirror	colour	the alphabet
bed	fridge	single/double	
sofa	washing machine	large/small	
(electric/gas) cooker	television		

SETTING UP
1. Ask half the class to look at the material for Student A and half the class to look at the material for Student B.
2. Tell the students to look at the cartoons at the top of their material. Ask:

What has he got?	(a washing machine)
Does he want it?	(no, he doesn't)
What does he want?	(an electric cooker)
What does *she* want? etc.	(a washing machine)
So...?	(they can exchange)

   Then ask students to barter what they've got with them in class with each other (books, pens, clothing which can (reasonably) be taken off, cigarettes, etc.). Start this off yourself by showing the students something you've got but don't want – as in the captions under the cartoons in their books.
   For example, hold up your pen and say 'I've got a beautiful pen. Does anyone want it?' When a student volunteers, ask him about what he's got in exchange. If you don't want it, say so, and ask him what else he's got, even suggesting things yourself ('Do you want your hat?'). The students then do this themselves. Insist that everyone exchanges *something*.
   Alternatively, they could barter things they have at home.
3. Ask students with the *same* material to work in pairs. They look at the forms in their material and discuss what each person wants and what he's got.
   Tell them to find out who can exchange with who in their material.
   (Each student should find one pair in his own material – see Solution.)
   Check that the students are using the structures and lexis correctly.
4. Bring the two halves of the class together in pairs and leave them to it.

MONITORING   Don't intervene. Leave the students to cope by themselves. Instead, watch for how well they communicate (see Introduction, section 6.5).

28

SOLUTION

In St.A's material, Peter Old and Sue Jones can exchange. In St.B's material, Tina Perry and Steve Evans can exchange. Between St.A and St.B, Carol Duncan (St.A) can exchange with Joan Palmer (St.B), and James Court (St.A) can exchange with Harry Brook (St.B).

HOMEWORK

Students write very simple letters to shops in an English-speaking country asking whether they've got certain items the students want. This could be in a business context, or for antiques or books, etc.

Ideas

PREPARATION
ACTIVITIES

Have got

Insurance   Students write down lists of everything someone can be insured for (house, car, boat, jewellery, camera, etc.) and invent a premium for each one.

In pairs, one student is the customer and the other is the insurance broker. The insurance broker asks his customer if he's got each thing on the list and works out the total premium. The customers go from one broker to another until they find the cheapest premium.

You could complicate matters by having the premiums vary according to size (or number of rooms) and age of the object (minus 10% per year).

Have got and to want

Wedding lists   Put the class into small groups. One student in each group is 'getting married'. The others think up possible presents for him or her (e.g. 'Do you want a ...?' 'No, I've already got that.') and make a list of the things he or she wants.

Each student then finds a partner from another group and decides with him what to give the person, e.g. 'She wants a ...' 'No, it's too expensive.' For the students who are 'getting married', this simply becomes 'I want a ...' 'No, sorry, it's too expensive.'

Shopping   Ask the students to make shopping lists with four or five items on them. In pairs, one student is the customer and the other is the shopkeeper. The customer asks for what he wants (e.g. 'Have you got a pen?') and the shopkeeper has to imagine two different sorts he can offer ('Yes sir. Do you want a blue pen or a black pen?').

FOLLOW UP

Give an example of a personal advertisement on the board, e.g. 'Washing machine, General Electric, 2 years old, good condition, £85.00 o.n.o., tel 421882.'

Ask students to think of something they've got and don't want, and write a similar ad for it. In turn, each student then tells the class 'I've got a (washing machine). Does anyone want it?' The other students then ask him about the make, age, and price and decide whether or not to buy it.

ROLE-PLAY
(WITH VIDEO)

Students phone up about a 'for sale' ad to ask about make, age, price, etc.

Type out an ad (e.g. 'Washing machine for sale. Tel. 24186'), stick it onto a small ads page in a newspaper, and draw a circle around it.

Film the improvisation along the lines suggested in the role-play for Activity 3. To vary the presentation you might *start* with a close-up of the ad, and/or have the second student walk in and answer the phone before he sits down.

9 TRAFFIC SIGNS

Notes

AIM   To practise *can* (permission) and giving directions.

SITUATION   The activity is a kind of puzzle. Each student has to get from one point on his map to another (by car), but he's only got some of the traffic signs which show one-way roads, etc. marked on his map.

He finds a route by asking his partner if he can or can't go down certain streets, e.g.:

St.A: Can I go down (Andrew Street)?
St.B: No, you can't.
St.A: Why not?
St.B: Because it's one-way.

STRUCTURES   *Can I* | *go down (Andrew Street)?*
               turn | *right* | *into (Andrew Street)?*
                      left |
               park in (Andrew Street)?

LEXIS   *to want   traffic sign   near   * + the traffic signs given in the
        *to drive   map   between   * students' material
                       theatre
                       accident

SETTING UP   1. Ask half the students to look at the material for Student A and half the students to look at the material for Student B.
2. Go through the traffic signs at the right of their material and make sure they understand what each one means.

    Have students with the *same* material work in pairs, to discuss how the traffic signs apply to the streets on their plans (i.e. which roads are one-way, where you can park, etc.).
3. Ask the class as a whole:

    Are all the signs on your map?   (no)
    Where are the other signs?   (on my partner's map)

    Ask St.A students:

    Where are you?   (at work)
    Where do you want to go?   (to the theatre)

Check that all students have found where work (W) and the theatre (Th) are on the map. Also check that St.B students have seen the note at the bottom of their material ('There's an accident...'). (So that they don't forget, tell St.B students to mark the position of the accident on their maps.)

    Bring the class together in pairs and leave them to it. Check that they follow the question and answer pattern suggested in Situation (above).
4. When St.A students have found their route, ask St.B students about where they are and where they want to go. Then leave them to it.

SOLUTION   St.A's route: George Street – Red House Street – Bath Road – Poor Lane
– car park in Hill Street behind the theatre.
St.B's route: Bridge Street – River Street – Exchange Road – Castle Road
(car park) – Castle Road – Exchange Road – Victoria Road –
High Road – Crown Street – Baker Lane – George Street – car
park in Brick Street.

HOMEWORK   Students draw a plan of their area. In the following class, each student explains
to the others which roads are one-way, etc.

Ideas

PREPARATION   *Can (permission)*
ACTIVITIES

Bedsit rules   Write the names of two bedsits on the board. Ask half the class
to imagine the rules for one of them and the other half to imagine the rules
for the other one. You might write a list of points on the board for them
to think about (e.g. smoking, dogs, visitors, etc.).

Bring the two halves of the class together in pairs. One of the students
is the landlord, the other is a tourist, and the tourist asks about the rules
('Can I...?'). Students then exchange roles.

Countries   Students guess which country or countries you're talking about
from the rules which you give for them, e.g. 'You can't drink whisky.' (Iran),
'You can't have two husbands.' (England, Germany, etc.), 'You can have
two husbands.' (Tibet), 'You can only have one child.' (China), 'You can't
drive on the right.', etc. Include ages for driving licences, women's rights,
etc. while preparing your list.

Directions

See the ideas for Activity 13.

ROLE-PLAY   Students discuss the best route to get from one place to another, using a map
(WITH VIDEO)   of an area which at least one of them knows well.

Put the camera quite close to the students. Start with a shot which takes
in both students and the map, then zoom slowly in on the map and follow
the student's hand tracing the route. Zoom out again when the students have
finished and are folding up the map.

10 LOVE-MATCH

Notes

AIM
To practise *can* (ability) and *to like*.

SITUATION
The Love-match Agency finds friends for its clients by putting them in touch with people who have similar – or complementary – likes, dislikes and abilities.

Each student has a letter from a new client and the record cards for two other clients. He fills in a record card for the new client, using the information in the letter.

He then finds the right friend for the client by comparing him or her with the other clients in his own and his partner's material. To do this, the students have to decide which differences of taste and/or ability matter, and which don't.

STRUCTURES
Can he play tennis?
Does he like going out?
Does it matter?
What (else) can he do?

LEXIS

to play	*tennis*	*Arabic*	*perhaps*
to speak	*guitar*	*Japanese*	*very well*
to draw	*journalist*	*French*	*a little*
to travel	*taxi driver*	*German*	*sometimes*
	salesman	*Spanish*	*very much*
	receptionist	*the same*	
	boy/girl-friend	*the right* (friend)	

SETTING UP
1. Ask half the class to look at the material for Student A and half the class to look at the material for Student B.
2. Ask students with the same material to work in pairs. One student works with the blank form and asks questions while the other scans the letter for the answers.

    If your students are unfamiliar with the technique of scanning, see Note on Scanning, Introduction, section 4.
3. Ask the class as a whole:

What does the Love–match Agency do?	(It helps you to find friends)
What is Anne Kato looking for?	(St.A: a boy-friend)
What is Housnu Kemal looking for?	(St.B: a girl-friend)
Is Bernardo the right friend for Anne?	
Is Bibi the right friend for Housnu?	

    Tell students to find out by comparing the abilities and likes of the two people. You may wish to ask two students (with the same material, as in step 2) to demonstrate this. The students discuss, rather than ask and answer questions, e.g.:

    'Anne can play tennis, and Bernardo can play tennis very well. That's OK ... Anne can speak French very well. Bernardo can't speak French, but it doesn't matter.'

When they've got the idea, tell the students to make a note of the problems, i.e. the differences which, in their opinion, matter.

Use this period to check that they're using the structures and lexis correctly, and help with problems. From time to time you might ask why a student thinks this or that difference matters.

4. Ask the students what problems they've found.

Then bring the two halves of the class together in pairs. Tell St.A students to find out about George Shipway and St.B students to find out about Hanna Buchner and note the problems. They should then choose the best boy or girl-friend for Anne and Housnu.

MONITORING   Don't intervene. Students should cope for themselves. Instead, watch for how well they communicate (see Introduction, section 6.5).

SOLUTION   Bernardo is probably the best boy-friend for Anne. The main problem is that he likes travelling while Anne doesn't. Students may also feel that age is a problem (Bernardo is younger than Anne).

Hanna is probably the best girl-friend for Housnu. The main problem is their different ideas of where to go out. They may also prove too competitive in sports.

HOMEWORK   Students write a letter to the agency about themselves.

Ideas

PREPARATION   *Can (ability)*
ACTIVITIES

Triathlon   Tell the students to imagine a sort of triathlon in which the men have to do three things (e.g. play tennis, sew, sing) and the women have to do three different things (e.g. swim, draw, make a cupboard). Students then go around asking each other how well they can do these things and decide which man and which woman could represent the class in the triathlon.

Can and like

Jobs   Write the names of a number of jobs on the board and ask the students to think of at least three abilities which are necessary for each of the jobs. In pairs, students then find out which jobs most suit each other by asking their partners if they can do these things *and* if they like doing them.

FOLLOW UP   Students fill in the form for each other and then find out who could get on with who in the class.

ROLE-PLAY   Students imagine they are two people who the agency has put in touch with
(WITH VIDEO)   each other, and they are meeting for the first time in a café.

At the beginning, have one student sit waiting, perhaps with a bunch of flowers. The other should approach him tentatively, unsure whether he's the one she's looking for or not. The improvisation ends when they decide to go somewhere else.

11 CALORIES

Notes

<dl></dl>

AIM To practise talking about height, age and weight; the use of *Would you like?* and *How many?*

SITUATION The students work out whether they are over or underweight and then go on to order a meal, taking into account the calorie content of their order.

  In the first part of the activity, Student A has a table showing the optimum weights for men and women depending on height, age and build. He asks Student B questions in order to find out whether St.B is the right weight or not.

  In the second part of the activity, St.A has the menu at the Elmtree Restaurant and chooses what he'd like to eat. St.B has a list of the calories in each item, so he can tell St.A if he's ordered too much or too little, depending on the number of calories St.A needs.

STRUCTURES

How | *old* | *are you?*
  | *tall* |
What's your weight?

What would you like?
How many calories are in the (rice)?
Please cancel the (rice). I'd like (peas) instead.

LEXIS

to order	*centimetres*	*right/wrong*	*+ the food items on the menu*
to need	*kilograms*	*over/under*	
to change			
to add/subtract			

SETTING UP 1. Divide the class into pairs. Ask all the students to look at the material for Student A and demonstrate the use of the table by asking one student the questions yourself.

  Ask one student in each pair to close his book while his partner asks him the questions to find out if he's the right weight or not. When they've finished the students exchange roles.

  2. Ask one student in each pair to turn to the material for Student B. Ask:

   Where are you?   (in the Elmtree Restaurant)
   For dinner?   (no, for lunch)
   What would you like to eat? (I'd like ...)

  Then have the students discuss with each other what they'd like to eat. Tell them to write down their orders.

  You may like to have them move their desks so that the classroom looks like a restaurant. Have them come into the 'restaurant', ask for a table, and improvise small talk.

  3. Ask a St.A student:

   How many calories do you need for lunch? (I don't know)
  Ask a St.B student:
   How many calories does he need?

34

St.B finds the answer in the instructions at the bottom of his material. Then ask the St.A. student:

How many calories are in your lunch?   (I don't know)

Tell him to ask St.B about the number of calories in each item he has ordered. Together they work out the total. If the result is too many or too few calories, tell the St.A student to change his order with help from St.B.

Make sure that the other students in the class follow what's happening throughout this stage.

4. If there are no problems, leave them to it.

HOMEWORK   Give your students conversion tables and have them work out their heights in feet and their weights in pounds (1 foot $\approx 30\frac{1}{2}$ cm, 1 inch $\approx 2\frac{1}{2}$ cm, 1 pound ≈ 445 grams).

Ideas

PREPARATION ACTIVITIES

How tall/old?, etc.

Passports   Students ask each other the questions needed to fill in the front (identity) page of a passport. The situation could be an application for a passport in a government office.

Casting   Ask half the students to guess the age, height and weight of the women on page 23 of their books, and the other half to do the same for the men on page 23. Tell them to make a note of their guesses. (You could use magazine pictures instead.)

Set the situation of a casting director who needs a man and a woman for a new film. Point out that the age and height of these people are very important. Then tell the first half (who have notes for the women) the director's specifications for the man, and the second half (with notes for the men) the specifications for the woman.

Bring the class together in pairs so they can work out which man and woman come closest to the couple the director is looking for. Students should not immediately tell their partners what height, age and weight they're looking for. Instead they should ask how tall, etc. each model is and then decide if he or she is too tall, etc.

Furniture   Adapt the 'Casting' idea above to choosing furniture. Give half the students pictures of various tables, perhaps on a duplicated sheet, and half the class pictures of cupboards, and have them guess how long, wide, much, etc. they are.

Then bring them together in pairs as customer and shop assistant. Tell the customer to decide the dimensions and maximum price of the table or cupboard he wants to buy and leave them to it.

FOLLOW UP   Students work out their British and US sizes for shoes and clothes.

	Women's clothes							Men's clothes			
British	10	12	14	16	18	20	22	37–38	39–40	41–42	43–44
Continental	38	40	42	44	46	48	50	94–97	99–102	104–107	109–112
American	8	10	12	14	16	18	20	38	40	42	44

	Women's shoes								Men's shoes						
British	3	4	5	6	7	8	9		7	8	9	10	11	12	13
Continental	35½	36½	38	39½	40½	42	43		41	42	43	44	45½	47	48
American	4½	5½	6½	7½	8½	9½	10½		8	9	10	11	12	13	14

ROLE-PLAY
(WITH VIDEO)

In groups of three or four, one student improvises guiding tourists (the other students) around his home town. Encourage the tourists to say what they think of the places the guide shows them, and to ask about height, age, etc. They could also calculate among themselves how much the dimensions are in feet and the prices in dollars or pounds.

Draw symbols to represent each place on pieces of paper (a wavy blue line could represent the Danube, for example) and stick them on the walls around the classroom. If your video camera is portable, follow the tourist party around the room with it.

12 RECIPES

Notes

AIM
To practise *How much/many?*, *have got* and *to need*.

SITUATION
Student A wants to make a pizza, Student B wants to make a salad. They each have a list of ingredients and a drawing of what they've already got in their kitchen.

Each student works out the things he still needs and then asks his partner for them.

STRUCTURES
Have you got | *any oil?*
Do you need |
How much oil | *have you got?*
How many olives | *do you need?*

LEXIS
pizza	*oil*	*tuna*	*teaspoon*
salad	*olives*	*vinegar*	*tablespoon*
flour	*mushrooms*	*mustard*	
yeast	*lettuce*		

SETTING UP
1. Ask half the class to look at the material for Student A and half the class to look at the material for Student B.
2. Ask:

   What do you want to make?   (St.A: a pizza)
                                (St.B: a salad)
   What do you need?   (St.A and St.B give the first few
                                things listed in their recipes)
   What have you got?   (St.A and St.B mention a few things
                                in the drawings)
   Have you got everything?   (I don't know)

3. Ask students with the *same* material to work in pairs, to find out what they still need. One student could look at the list of ingredients ('Have we got 500g of flour?') while the other looks at the drawing ('No, we've (only) got 200g, so we (still) need 300g.').

   Tell the students to make a list of everything they still need.

   Use this period to check that the students are using the structures and lexis correctly, and help with any problems.
4. Bring the two halves of the class together in pairs, and tell the students to ask their partners for the things they still need.

   If you like, have the students improvise knocking on their 'neighbour's' door, with 'Sorry to bother you, but . . .', etc.

MONITORING
When the students have finished, ask them what they still need to buy from the shops – St.A needs 12 black olives and 100g of ham, St.B needs 150g of tuna, 1 potato and 100g of cheese. (*Note:* students can only give their partner what they've got spare, e.g. St.B has got some ham, but he needs it himself.)

Don't intervene. Students should cope by themselves. Instead, watch for how well they communicate (see Introduction, section 6.5).

HOMEWORK   Students find a recipe they like, or invent one, and write down the list of ingredients. In the next class, each student reads out his list. The others have to guess what kind of dish it is (cake, soup, etc.)* and invent a name for it.

* Don't pre-teach words like 'stew', 'pie' or whatever. Simply have a dictionary on hand for the students to look them up themselves.

Ideas

PREPARATION   *How much/many?, have got and need*
ACTIVITIES
Supermarket stock check   Make out a list of twelve items showing how much or many of each item the supermarket needs for the coming month. Make out another list showing how much/many of each item the supermarket already has in stock. Duplicate the lists according to how many pairs of students you have in your class.

In pairs, each student has one of the lists. Together they work out what they need to order for the next month ('We've got 50kg of flour. How much do we need?' 'We need 70kg.' 'So we still need 20kg.').

Shopping lists   Write a list of about ten food items on the board. Ask students to choose five items which they need to buy and note the quantity of each item they need. They should imagine that they've got the other five items.

In pairs, one student imagines he is about to go to the supermarket, and asks the other 'Do you need any ...?' ('No, I've got enough'), etc. The student should make a list of the things his partner needs, so he can check it with his partner when they've finished.

Playing cards   Distribute a pack of playing cards among the students, and tell them they each have to get three of a kind, or a run of four cards in the same suit. To do this, they exchange cards with other students in the class. They do not look at each other's cards, but ask 'Have you got ...?' '(What) do you need ...?', etc. and they must exchange, not simply give the cards to one another.

The vocabulary is a little specialized, so simply write the names of the suits and 'ace', etc. on the board for the students to refer to.

The first person to get three of a kind or a run wins. Then shuffle the cards, and let them do it again.

FOLLOW UP   With *chop, slice, mix, cook, fry, put*, the students should be able to explain recipes from their native countries to each other.

ROLE-PLAY   Students improvise asking their neighbours for things.
(WITH VIDEO)   If you have the student go out and knock on the door of the classroom, the whole improvisation could be shot from the neighbour's point of view.

Put the things for the neighbour to give on a table and let him go out of camera shot to get them while the student waits at the door.

If you haven't got food items in class, the student could ask for chairs, a bulb, typing paper, etc.

13 LOST IN SPA

Notes

AIM   To practise describing the positions of streets and buildings, and giving directions.

SITUATION   Student A and Student B give each other directions, using a plan of Spa.
Each student has a route to help him prepare the directions he will give his
partner. His directions should include both street names and landmarks.

  When they start working in pairs, the student who asks for directions will
discover that some of the streets and landmarks are not marked on his map,
so he has to ask where they are. For example;
  St.A: Turn right into School Road.
  St.B: Where's School Road?
  St.A: It's opposite the telephone box.
  St.B: Hmm. OK.

The Reading Passage on page 10 of the Student's Book accompanies this
activity. It's a letter from Alan, who lives in Spa, to Anna, who is coming
to visit him. Students scan the letter to find the directions from Spa Station
to Alan's house. Both St.A and St.B have the streets and landmarks needed
for this marked on their maps.

STRUCTURES   *How do I get to (the tennis courts)?*
Go| down (Union Road).
* | past (the library).*
Turn | right | into (Union Road).
* | left | at (the library).*
Cross (Union Road).

LEXIS | | |
|---|---|
| *telephone box* | *opposite* |
| *car park* | *next to* |
| *church* | *between* |
| *YMCA* | *on the corner* |
| *landmark* | |

SETTING UP   1. Ask half the class to look at the material for Student A and half the class
to look at the material for Student B.
  2. *The reading passage*: If you wish, have the students do the reading passage
on page 10 of their books at this point, to familiarize them with the map.
If your students are not used to this technique, see Note on Scanning,
Introduction, section 4.
    Point out that Anna is coming by train (so the directions start from the
station) and that Alan is giving her directions to his house. The students
should mark Alan's house on their maps when they've found it (at the
end of the small street between Royal Park and the river).
  3. *The activity*: Ask the students to look at the instructions at the bottom
of their material. Ask:
      Where are you?   (St.A: at Spa Station)
                                    (St.B: at the Holbourne Museum)

⫸→

Where do you want to go?   (St.A: to the tennis courts)
(St.B: to the Technical College)

4. Ask students with the *same* material to work in pairs, and prepare the directions they will give their partners later in the activity. Point out that they should follow the route given and include both street names and landmarks in their directions.

   Use this period to check on their use of the structures and lexis, and help with any problems.

5. Bring the two halves of the class together in pairs and leave them to it.

MONITORING   The students will be strongly tempted to look at each other's material or ask for clarification in their native language. If this happens, stop them and insist that they resolve *everything* in English.

   Students should not start labelling the missing names on their plans. The objective is only to get to the correct destination.

HOMEWORK   Students write a letter to a friend giving directions from the local train or bus station to their house.

Ideas

PREPARATION
ACTIVITIES

Prepositions

The town centre   Draw a plan like this one on the board and ask the students to copy it twice (or prepare copies for them if you have access to a duplicator).

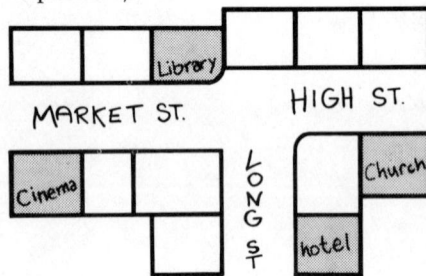

Note that each blank space can be described in relation to one of the named facilities with *next to* and *opposite*.
Write a list of eight more facilities (bank, pub, etc.) on the board, and tell the students to fill in the blank spaces on one of their plans with them, in whatever arrangement they like.

In pairs, each student then asks his partner about his arrangement and copies it on his other plan (e.g. 'Where's the pub?' 'It's opposite the cinema in Market Street.').

Directions

Landmarks   On the board, draw a route with the street names through a well-known part of the city you're teaching in. Ask the students to think of the landmarks along the way. Then have one student give you the directions so that you can answer like this:

Student: Go down Market Street.
You: Past Lloyd's Bank?
Student: Yes, that's right. And turn left into Adam Street.
You: At the supermarket?
Student: Yes.

When they've got the idea, students can invent their own routes to try out on each other.

13: Lost in Spa

Bus routes   Bring in information pamphlets which give the routes through the city you're teaching in. In small groups, one student dictates a bus route while the others trace it on an ordinary plan of the city.

FOLLOW UP

Sketch a plan of the streets around your school on the board and fill in as many of the street names and landmarks as you and your students can remember. Students then give each other directions to shops, restaurants, etc. which they recommend in the area.

ROLE-PLAY
WITH VIDEO)

Asking for directions in the street: Give one student (a tourist) a map and tell another student (a local resident) to think of something he can be doing in the street (repairing a car, feeding pigeons, etc.). Have the tourist stand fairly close to the camera, with the local resident in the background (out of focus).

The tourist consults his map, and then looks around as if he's trying to find out where he is, consults his map again, etc. Then he 'notices' the resident and starts walking towards him. At the same moment, change the focus onto the resident. Keep this picture until the tourist walks off in the direction the resident has just pointed out.

14 STAGE PLAN

Notes

AIM   To practise the use of simple prepositions and adjectives.

SITUATION   The students plan the stage set for two scenes of a play. They need to know what each prop (piece of furniture) is like, and where it goes on the stage.

Each student has the stage directions for one scene and has to ask his partner about the other scene.

STRUCTURES   *What's the table like?*
Where is it?

LEXIS

wardrobe	low	near	in the centre
bookcase	heavy/light	behind	next to
cushions	hard/soft	in front of	between
	round/square	opposite	
	uncomfortable		

SETTING UP
1. Ask half the class to look at the material for Student A and half the class to look at the material for Student B.
2. Ask:

Where do you work?	(in the theatre)
What's the name of the play?	(*Fire and the Waters*)
What are these?	(the instructions)
For which scene?	(St.A: Act 1, Scene 1)
	(St.B: Act 2, Scene 3)

You may wish to discuss the meanings of *act, scene, stage, stage directions* and *props* with the students at this point.

If you feel it necessary to explain USC (upstage centre), DSR and DSL (downstage right and left), point out that in the theatre the part of the stage near the audience is called downstage, and the part away from the audience is called upstage. Left and right are considered from the actor's point of view.

Ask St.A students:

Is there a table in Act 1, Scene 1?	(yes)
What's it like?	(it's heavy and round)
Where is it?	(it's next to the window)

Go through the same set of questions for St.B students: 'Is there a bed on the stage in Act 2, Scene 3?' They should answer 'yes', 'new, double' and 'next to the bookcase' respectively.
3. Have students with the *same* material work in pairs. One student looks at the props list, and asks 'Is there a TV?' 'What's it like?', etc. while the other scans the text for the answers.

The students should not write anything during this stage.

Use this period to check on the students' use of the structures and lexis and help with any problems.
4. Bring the two halves of the class together in pairs, and ask:

What has your partner got?   (St.A: The directions for Act 2, Scene 3)
(St.B: The directions for Act 1, Scene 1)
Point out that they should draw the props in the correct position on their stage plans, and make notes on what they're like. Then leave them to it.

MONITORING   At the end of the activity you could ask students to find out why the props have changed so drastically. If they scan the stage directions for Act 2, Scene 3 they will find that there is a fire at the end of Act 2, Scene 2.
Don't intervene. Students should cope for themselves. Instead, watch for how well they communicate (see Introduction section 6.5).

SOLUTION

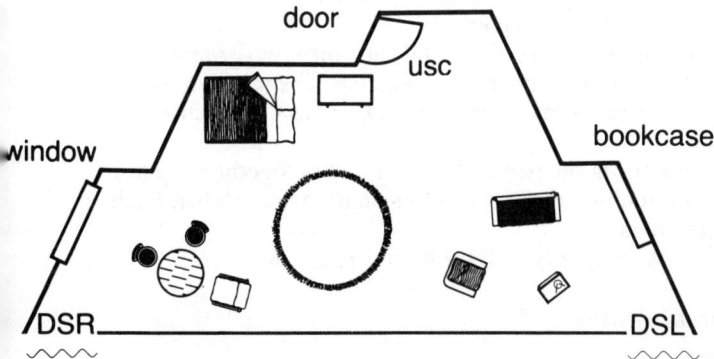

STAGE PLAN: ACT 1, SCENE 1

Props List   Act *1* Scene *1*

bed   large, double
Wardrobe   heavy
T·V   —
Sofa   small, uncomfortable
armchair   large soft
table   heavy, round, wooden
chairs   2 hard uncomfortable
          1 low, soft
carpet   round
cushions   —

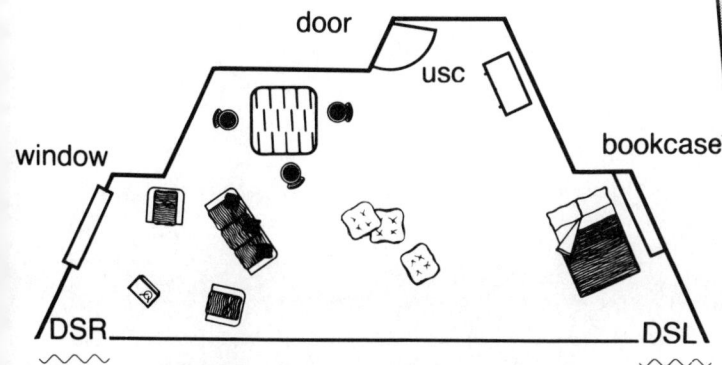

STAGE PLAN: ACT 2, SCENE 3

Props List   Act *2* Scene *3*

bed   new, double
Wardrobe   small light
T·V   small colour
sofa   long, low, comfortable
armchair   2-low, comfortable
table   large square
chairs   2-3 hard
carpet   —
cushions   3 or 4 large

⟫⟫→

43

HOMEWORK Students write a note to a friend listing half a dozen things they want this friend to get from their house, with directions on how to find them, e.g. 'My car keys – they're in the top drawer of the large wooden desk behind the sofa in the living room.'

Ideas

PREPARATION ACTIVITIES *What's it like?*

The tourist office   The students select where to go on holiday, e.g. choosing which Greek island to go to before leaving Athens.

Before the class, write down the details for two possible places on a sheet of paper (hotels, beaches, countryside, prices, etc.) and the details for two different places on a second sheet of paper.

Write the four names on the board, divide the class into two groups, and give one of the sheets to one student in each group. The other students (the tourists) ask him (the tourist office) what the two places on his list are like, and take notes.

When they've finished, bring the two halves of the class together in pairs so that each student can find out about the places on his partner's list. Each pair then decides where to go.

The activity could be used equally well for hotels, restaurants, etc.

What's it like? and prepositions

See the Ideas for Activity 13.

Rooms   Students draw outlines of a room in their house and next to this outline list the furniture in the room. In pairs, each student gives his outline and list to his partner. His partner then uses the list to ask where each piece of furniture is, and what it is like. He then draws it onto the outline.

FOLLOW UP Bring in genuine play texts for the students to work with. They should be able to understand the general outline of the stage set for a large number of twentieth-century plays.

15 THE WEATHER

Notes

AIM   To practise talking about the weather, agreeing and disagreeing.

SITUATION   The students have three different weather forecasts: BBC television (St.A), ITV
television (St.B), and the *Daily Echo* newspaper (St.B). Each forecast gives
the weather conditions for seven major cities in the United Kingdom, but they
don't all agree.

   The students compare the ITV and the BBC forecasts. When they don't
agree on the weather conditions for a particular city, St.B scans the *Daily
Echo* article to find out which forecast it confirms – the BBC or ITV. St.A
marks the weather conditions which are confirmed on his map.

STRUCTURES   *What's the weather like in (Aberdeen)?*
Do you agree?

LEXIS   *snowing   sunny   hot*
raining   cloudy   cold
*   windy*
*   foggy*

SETTING UP   1. Ask half the class to look at the material for Student A and half the class
to look at the material for Student B.
   If you wish, have students with the *same* material work in pairs to
practise asking each other about the weather. They should use only the
TV forecast in their material.
2. Ask:
       What have you got?   (St.A: the BBC weather forecast)
                             (St.B: the ITV weather forecast and the *Daily Echo*
                                 forecast)
   You might briefly compare these with television channels and newspapers
in the students' own countries.
3. Bring the two halves of the class together in pairs. Tell the students to
check the BBC and the ITV forecasts together, and explain that if they
don't agree, St.B should scan the *Daily Echo* article to see what it says.
   You might introduce the phrase 'according to (the BBC)' before the
students begin.
   Note: It is possible to do this activity in groups of four: one student works with
the blank map in St. A's material (and asks the questions) while the other three have
one forecast each. For a group of three, split the St.B rather than the St.A
material.

MONITORING   There is no reason why students shouldn't decide to keep both weather
conditions for a particular town, if they are close enough (e.g. it could be
windy and raining in Belfast).
   Don't intervene. Students should cope for themselves. Instead, watch for
how well they communicate (see Introduction, section 6.5).

45

SOLUTION

HOMEWORK   Students watch the weather forecast that evening on TV and write a simple newspaper article about it.

   If you assign different channels to different students they could compare in the next lesson to see if there is any conflict between the forecasts.

Ideas

PREPARATION
ACTIVITIES

What's it like?

See the Ideas for Activity 14.

TV Forecasts   Sketch a large map of the country you're teaching in on the board, with the major cities marked on it.

   Students then improvise giving TV weather forecasts. One student gives the commentary while the other draws the symbols on the map.

   You might ask them to substitute *will be* for *is*.

Confirming opinions (agreeing)

Lists   Write out three lists. Each list has six statements about different topics, but they don't all agree. For example, the first statement on list 1 could be 'Tripoli is in the north of Lebanon', but on list 2 this might be 'Tripoli is in the south of Lebanon', and on list 3 'Tripoli is in the north of Lebanon.' Make sure that each time, there are two lists which agree.

   Divide the class into groups of three and give a set of lists to each group. One student in each group begins by reading out the first statement on his list. The other two students then agree or disagree with it. At the end of the activity each group should be able to compile a 'definitive' list made up of the statements for which two of the lists agree.

FOLLOW UP   Students each bring in a different morning paper to see if they agree on the weather forecast (or horoscope?!).

16 TIMETABLES

Notes

AIM   To practise the Simple Present in the context of opening times, departure times, etc.

SITUATION   The students are on holiday in Farnmouth at Mrs Lowe's guest house. They have to plan the last day of their holiday together, using the information on the guest house notice board, a letter from Mrs Lowe and other notices.

Each student has a note showing what he wants to do. He plans his day as far as possible, and then adjusts his programme with his partner so that they can both do everything.

STRUCTURES   *What time does the bank open?*
I want to change my traveller's cheques.
Let's go to the bank at 10.30.

LEXIS
to open	*to buy*	*museum*	the days of the week
to close	*to go*	*concert*	telling the time
to start	*to visit*		
to finish	*to see*	*a.m./p.m.*	
to leave	*to change*		
to arrive			

SETTING UP
1. Ask half the class to look at the material for Student A and half the class to look at the material for Student B.
2. Ask all the students:
Where are you?	(in Farnmouth)
At a hotel?	(no, at Mrs Lowe's guest house)
What day is it?	(Sunday)
When does your train leave?	(at 9.45 tomorrow morning)
What do you want to do today?	(St.A and St.B start reading out their notes)
When can you see *What a Wallop*?	(St.A: at 7.50 or 10.00)
When can you go to the concert?	(St.B: at 1.30)
3. You may find it useful to run briefly through the two lists of what the students want to do, asking 'Who's got information about (banks)?', etc. so that the students are aware that they'll have to ask their partners for some of the information. Then ask students with the *same* material to work in pairs and plan their day as far as possible. Encourage them to ask each other and answer questions about opening times, departure times, etc. for other things in their material as well.

   Use this period to check on their use of the structures and lexis and help with any problems.
4. Bring the two halves of the class together in pairs. Tell the students to ask their partner about when they can do the other things on the list, e.g. ask St.A:
When can you buy food for lunch?	(St.A: I don't know)
Ask your partner.	

   and point out that they should plan their day *together*. Then leave them to it.

MONITORING Some students naturally have problems organizing a timetable in their own language. If this happens, suggest that they make a common list of the things they want to do, and write down the possible times for each next to each item. A second step would be to divide these into things to do in the morning, afternoon and evening.

Otherwise, don't intervene. Students should cope for themselves. Watch for how well they communicate (see Introduction, section 6.5).

SOLUTION Morning: Bank (10.30), supermarket (11.00?), museum (12.00?).
Afternoon: Concert (1.30–2.30), beach (first bus after the concert leaves Green Park 2.45) (last bus back, if they want to see the film at 7.50, leaves Long Beach 7.15).
Evening: *What a Wallop* (7.50), the Mandarin Restaurant (10.00) (unless they eat first, and see the film at 10.00), the Cavern disco (12.00).

HOMEWORK Students write a letter to a friend who is going to stay at their house while they, the students, are away on holiday. The letter gives details of shops, buses and trains in their area.

Ideas

PREPARATION
ACTIVITIES

Opening times, departure times, etc.

In each of the following activities, you must prepare a simple information sheet before class. The students work in small groups. One student in each group has a copy of the information sheet, and the others ask him for the information they need.

The right cinema

Information sheet: An entertainments guide or a sheet with the programmes for half a dozen cinemas.

Write the names of two or three films on the board. The students in each group choose one of them and a time they want to see it. They then ask the student in their group who has the information sheet about where it's showing and the time it starts in each cinema, until they find a cinema which suits them.

The right shops

Information sheet: a list of different kinds of shops near the school (e.g. butcher, baker), where they are, and their opening and closing times.

Write a shopping list on the board and ask the students to copy it. Then ask them what time they come to class or go to work and tell them they must do this shopping either before or after class (or work). They ask the student with the information sheet about the shops near the school (e.g. 'Are there any bakers near here?') and the times they open and close, until they find somewhere they can get each item on their list.

The right train

Information sheet: a list of departure times for trains to various cities. You could include information about platform numbers and arrival times.

On the board, write the names of three or four towns and draw a clock with any time you like on it. Explain that the clock shows the time now.

The students in each group choose a destination and ask the student with the information sheet what time the *next* train to it leaves. They can repeat the activity as often as you change the time on the clock.

Let's, I want to, opening times

Plans   Write a list of eight to ten things to do on the board. Each of them should depend on places being open or closed, departures, etc. (e.g. bank, shopping, church, film, boat ride, etc.). Ask students to work in pairs and decide which of these things they'd like to do today and which they'd like to do tomorrow.

When they've finished, ask one student to decide what the opening times for the bank today and tomorrow are, another to decide on film times, etc. Students then go around asking each other about these times. Then they return to their original pairs and finalize their plans for the two days.

FOLLOW UP   Students discuss what banks they go to, which supermarkets, restaurants, clubs, etc. in their area stay open late, which programmes they watch on TV and how they get to work.

17 NEIGHBOURS

Notes

AIM   To practise using the Simple Present to express habitual actions.

SITUATION   In an apartment building in San Francisco, two families who live in neighbouring apartments each have such different life-styles that they regularly disturb each other with noise. In another part of the building, two other families are having similar problems.

     The students decide whether the problem would be solved if the families exchanged apartments, and if so, who should exchange with who.

STRUCTURES   *What do they do in the morning?*
What time does he get up?
Does he sleep well?
When are they noisy?

LEXIS

to go for a walk	*nightclub*	*unemployed*	telling the time
to cry	*violin*	*retired*	
to go jogging		*quiet*	
		noisy	

(*Note:* Since this is in America, *do the housework* becomes *do the chores*.)

SETTING UP   1. Ask half the class to look at the material for Student A and half the class to look at the material for Student B.
2. Ask:

What are the names of your families?	(St.A: the Browns/the Johnsons) (St.B: the Allens/the Ketchams)
Where do they live?	(in San Francisco)
Are they neighbours?	(St.A: yes, the Johnsons live above the Browns) (St.B: yes, the Allens live above the Ketchams)
What's the problem?	(St.A: the Browns say . . ., etc.) (St.B: the Allens say . . ., etc.)

3. Ask students with the *same* material to work in pairs and find out when there are noise problems between the families.

     Each student works with the description of one of the families. Since these descriptions are all written in much the same way, they can compare point by point. For example, if a student reads that the Browns 'get up at 6.00' he should ask his partner 'What time do the Johnsons get up?'

     Stronger students should work with the Student B material since the comparisons there are not quite as straightforward.

     Students should note the problem times in the box provided as they come across them.

     Use this period to check on their use of the structures and lexis and help with any problems.

4. Discuss with the class when noise problems arise between the two sets of neighbours. Then point out that the families can exchange apartments.
   Bring the two halves of the class together in pairs and tell the students to find out who can live with who.
   Note: This activity works best with four students, each of whom works with one family.

MONITORING   If the students are having organizational problems, point out that the times when their families are noisy (or need quiet) are the important ones to ask their partner about, e.g. 'Mark Johnson is noisy in the afternoon. He plays the violin. What do your families do in the afternoon?'
   Otherwise, don't intervene. Students should cope for themselves. Watch for how well they communicate (see Introduction, section 6.5).

SOLUTION   The Ketchams and the Browns should exchange apartments.

HOMEWORK   Students write a letter complaining to their landlord about their neighbour — or from one of the people in the activity to his or her landlord.

Ideas

PREPARATION
ACTIVITIES   *Habitual actions*

Evening classes   Ask students to choose an evening class or sport for themselves which they don't already do (e.g. judo, painting, etc.).
   In pairs, one student then plays the receptionist of the school or sports centre, depending on his partner's choice. Together, they work out how to fit four hours a week of classes or sport into the student's schedule. Insist that the students treat the activity as real and find a time which is genuinely possible for them.
   If this proves too easy, tell students to add yet another evening class to their week.

Personalities   Give the students a number of topics and ask them to write down details about themselves for each topic. The topics can be as serious ('What kind of magazine do you read?') or frivolous ('Do you talk to machines?') as you like.
   When they've finished, collect their papers and read them out to the class one by one. At the end of each one, the students try to guess who has written it.

FOLLOW UP   Each student finds out which of the other students he could stand as neighbours and which he couldn't.

ROLE-PLAY
(WITH VIDEO)   One or two of the students are staying at the home of another student for the night. The student shows his guests their room, checks that they have got everything they need, and explains what time the family gets up, has breakfast, etc. before saying goodnight.
   Use your classroom door as the door into the bedroom. Place your camera facing the door but one or two metres to the right or left of it. If it's directly opposite or at 90 degrees to the door, the students are bound to get between each other and the camera (unless they naturally make sure they're always in the limelight!).

18   THE HOUSING COMMITTEE

Notes

AIM To practise using the Simple Present (personal identity/general states) with *there is* and *it is*.

SITUATION The students work for the Housing Committee of the City Council in Cambourne, Australia.

Three people have applied for flats. The students fill in official forms for them using the information provided in a letter from each person and the notes from a social worker who has met them. They then choose a flat or house for each applicant from the five places they have to offer.

STRUCTURES *What's his address?*
What does he do?
How much does he earn?
Has he got any dependants?
Is there a lift?
Is it furnished?

LEXIS
to need	*salary*	*first, second, etc.*
to earn	*rent*	*(un)furnished*
to pay	*suburb*	
	ground floor	*half a mile away*
	aunt	

SETTING UP 1. Ask all the students to look at the material for St.A and St.B on page 46, and fill in the form at the bottom of the page with the information in the letter at the top. (The letter should be scanned, not read word by word. If your students are not familiar with this technique, see Note on Scanning, Introduction, section 4.)

Either treat this as a reading comprehension for the students to do individually, or ask the questions yourself (or get the students to ask the questions) and have the class fill in the form together.

2. Ask the students to look at the houses and flats on page 48 and decide which one to give Yuon Hou.

3. Divide the class into pairs. In each pair, one student looks at the material for St.A (page 45) and the other looks at the material for St.B (page 47). Ask:

Where do you work?   (for the City Council Housing Committee)
What does the committee do?   (it helps people to find flats and houses)
You've got letters from two
    people. Who are they?   (St.A: Anne Littleton and Harry Marden)

Then tell the students to fill in the form for them and find them suitable accommodation. Students could exchange roles when they've filled in the form and found accommodation for one of the applicants.

Note: You could do this activity with groups of three, with one student working exclusively with the flats and houses on page 48.

MONITORING   For Anne Littleton's nationality, you may have to point out that Sydney is in Australia.

    Don't intervene. Students should cope for themselves. Instead, watch for how well they communicate (see Introduction, section 6.5).

SOLUTION   There is no perfect solution.

HOMEWORK   Students write a letter to the Housing Committee about themselves.

Ideas

PREPARATION
ACTIVITIES

Personal identity

See the ideas for Activity 3.

Tax forms   If you can, get hold of a number of local tax forms (or invent your own) and have the students fill them in for each other. This will cover points concerning dependants, earnings, other incomes, etc.

    Since income is usually a sensitive subject, have the students imagine the details for a fictional character rather than give their own details. You could give each student a picture of someone from a magazine or a role card for this.

    Insist that they should fill it in for a typical year, not last year, unless you want them to practise the simple past.

Talking about flats and houses

For sale   Students try to sell their flats or houses to each other. You might introduce this activity by asking them to note what is convenient or inconvenient about their present flat or house, taking its location and the facilities nearby into account. This will remind them of what to look for in a new flat, and suggest the qualities in their present flat which they should bring out when they're trying to sell it.

FOLLOW UP   Students discuss which of the houses or flats on offer in the activity they could live in, and explain why they could or couldn't live in each one.

ROLE-PLAY
(WITH VIDEO)   Five students simulate a meeting of the Housing Committee. One student is the chairman, another is in charge of the available accommodation, and the three others each present the case of one of the families who are looking for a flat.

    Each case should be presented very briefly so that the discussion on which flat to allocate to the family can start as soon as possible. Insist that the committee members do not speak unless the chairman has asked them to do so.

    If you want the whole class to participate, up to five students could be responsible for the flats (one each), and two or more students could present the case for each family.

    Have the students sit around a table with the chairman at one end of it. The camera should be a few metres from the other end, opposite the chairman. You may have to rearrange them as shown in the diagram below to make sure they're evenly spaced in the camera picture.

        ⟫→

Note the two people next to the chairman are sitting at the *corners* rather than the side of the table, and the others with their chairs further back the nearer they are to the camera.

19 HEALTH QUIZ

Notes

AIM
To practise using the Simple Present with *How often/many?* and frequency adverbs.

SITUATION
The students each have half of a magazine quiz about health.
They each do half of the quiz for themselves and then ask their partner the same questions, so that by the end, both students have answered all the questions. They then total up their points to find out whether their scores are positive or negative.

STRUCTURES
How often do you see the doctor?
Do you ever take sleeping pills?
How many cigarettes do you smoke a day?

LEXIS
to add	*rarely*	*more*
to subtract	*never*	
	sometimes	
quiz	*once*	
	twice	
	three times	

SETTING UP,
1. Ask half the students to look at the material for Student A and half the students to look at the material for Student B.
2. Ask students with the *same* material to work out the quiz questions and try them out on each other. Remind them to make a note of their scores.
   Use this period to check on their use of the structures and lexis and to help with any problems.
3. Bring the two halves of the class together in pairs and tell the students to ask each other their questions.

MONITORING
When they've finished, ask them to total up their scores to find out if the results are positive or negative.
Don't intervene. Students should cope for themselves.

HOMEWORK
Students prepare their own questionnaires. These could be on subjects of their own choice, or you could propose a subject such as finding out someone's social class or life-style, e.g. 'How often do you drink champagne?'

Ideas

PREPARATION
ACTIVITIES
Frequency adverbs

Adapt the 'Agreeing' idea in Activity 15 for statements using *always, sometimes, never,* etc.

⟫→

Preferences   Students discuss which shops they go to (or never go to) how often they go there, and say why they only sometimes, often or always go to them. They could have similar discussions about TV programmes, the kind of films they go to, books and magazines they read, etc.

Sexism   Ask the women in your class to work out a questionnaire which will reveal how sexist the men are. The questions could be based on how often they contribute to the housework, how often they listen to women's opinions on current events, etc.

In the meantime, the men prepare a questionnaire which will try to determine how liberated the women are.

When they've tried the questionnaire out on each other, have a class discussion about the justice of the questions (e.g. should a question like 'How often do you wear perfume?' in the men's questionnaire be allowed?).

The doctor   Divide the class into two halves. Tell one half they are doctors and tell the other half they are going to see the doctor because they feel tired all the time. In their groups, both doctors and patients think about why someone is tired all the time. The doctors prepare questions and the patients decide on what they should tell the doctor. When they're ready, bring the class together in pairs.

The roles can be reversed later, with the situation of someone who doesn't sleep well.

FOLLOW UP   On the basis of their questionnaire results, students decide what they should do to improve their health – and then admit to what they would actually be prepared to do.

ROLE-PLAY (WITH VIDEO)   Students play researchers stopping people on the street to ask them various questions about their life-style. The questionnaire could be a shortened version of the questionnaire in the activity, or one for a marketing survey, (e.g. 'Have you got a washing machine? How often do you use biological powder? Do you ever try new makes of washing powder?', etc.). The questionnaire should start with questions about the person's job and family situation.

Give the researcher a clipboard and have the other students walk up and down the room around the researcher to give the impression of a busy pavement. The researcher stops people as they go past. Remind the students that they can refuse to stop and answer the researcher.

If your video camera is portable, you, or one of your students, could stand beside the researcher with it, as if it's part of the interview. Try taking the class into one of the streets around your school for this.

20 STAR SIGNS

Notes

AIM

To practise using the Simple Present and *to be*: general revision.

SITUATION

Students work out which of the four element signs corresponds best to their partner's character. They then go on to work out their partner's star sign. They also decide how well their own star sign describes their character and explain why they think it does or doesn't.

STRUCTURES

Are they interested in religion?
How often do you change your ideas?
Are you ever romantic?
I (don't) think so.

LEXIS

Element signs:	Star signs:	jealous
to spend (time)	to control	funny
		afraid
order	crowds	honest
life	art	wonderful
	science	ambitious
impatient	imagination	logical
romantic		charming
enthusiastic		intelligent
		modern
carefully		lazy

what kind of . . .?

Note: Students only need to understand these words. Pre-teach the element sign lexis, but leave the star sign lexis to explain as and when the students need it.

SETTING UP

Element signs

1. Ask all the students to look at the page about element signs.
   Begin with a brief discussion like the one suggested at the top of the page, by asking the students if they're romantic, etc. Then ask them to tell you what Earth or Air people (for example) are like.
2. Select a student and ask the class if they think he or she is an Earth or Air person (depending on what you choose at the end of step 1).
   The class then ask the student the questions for that element one by one. After each question the students should think up one or two more questions to elicit further information (e.g. 'Are you impatient?' 'No, I'm not.' 'Are you ever impatient?' 'Yes, but rarely.' 'What are you impatient about?' . . .).
   At the end, the students assess whether or not the element corresponds to the person's character.
3. Briefly go through the points for the other elements, asking the students

⟫→

to suggest a few further questions for each (see below). This is only to give them ideas, so it should go quickly, and the students shouldn't write anything.

4. Divide the class into small groups of four or five. Tell them to find the best sign for each member of the group, and leave them to it.

Star signs   (this could be done in the following lesson)

1. All the students look at the page about star signs.

Select one student and ask him which element sign he is. Then ask how many star signs there are for that element (three) and what they are.

Have the class ask the student the questions for those signs one by one. Unlike step 2 for the element signs (see above) they should ask only the occasional further question, so that it doesn't take too long.

At the end, assess which sign the student should be, according to his answers, and find out what his real sign is. If the two signs are not the same, ask him if he thinks his real sign fits him or not, and to explain why.

Warning: Some students will take one look at the page and say 'Oh, I'm a ... What are you?', so be prepared to tell them to wait and see if the others can find out.

2. Divide the students into small groups of four or five and leave them to continue by themselves.

You may wish to bring the class back together for the final discussion about how well their real signs fit.

Ideas for further questions   (Element signs)

Fire   What are you enthusiastic about?
Which newspaper do you read?
or: Are you interested in all
religions?
Do you make a lot of mistakes?
Are you always impatient?

Air   Are you often bored?
Do you have any very good friends?
Do you finish everything you start?
or: Are your ideas always good ones?
What do you do in your spare time?
or: How much time do you spend with your
family?

Earth   Are you patient in a traffic jam?
Do you work alone in your job?
When do you plan your summer
holiday?
Is it easy to live with you?

Water   Do you enjoy fairy stories/
science fiction?
Do you cry in the cinema?
When are you happy?
Is your flat usually in a mess?

In general, the students should come up with their own questions. These, and your own ideas, should only be used it they get *really* stuck.

HOMEWORK   The students describe themselves and the kind of people they get on with well. A context for this could be a letter to a computer dating agency (see Activity 10) or a letter to a friend explaining why they're getting on fabulously with a new friend or why they've broken up with an old one.

Alternatively, the students write a magazine column giving an 'exclusive', 'scandalous' character portrait of a TV or film personality or other public figure.

Ideas

PREPARATION
ACTIVITIES

The lexis used in the activity

Happy families   Bring in pictures of four or five people and tell the students
these people are the members of the same family, and live in the same house.
Discuss the character traits for each person with the students, bringing in
the activity lexis as well as the students' own contributions. Get the students
to give you one or two examples of the things each person does for each
of his or her traits. When you've finished, ask the students to imagine when
and why different members of the family get angry with each other.

Follow this up with a discussion of people in the students' own families
who they get on with well, or don't get on with at all, and why.

FOLLOW UP

Extend the examples the students give of how well or badly the description
of their element or star sign corresponds to their character by bringing in
other tenses, depending on your students' level. This could be the Simple Past,
through anecdotes; the Present Perfect, covering their lives so far; or *used
to* for tendencies which they've got rid of.

21 THE DEPARTMENT STORE

Notes

AIM To practise using the Present Continuous for present actions.

SITUATION The department store in the activity has a double security system; detectives on the shop floor and video cameras. A video controller spots a shoplifter and tells a detective about her. The detective follows her, but keeps losing sight of her, and he has to call the video controller back to find out what she's doing each time.

Student A is the video controller; Student B is the shop detective.

STRUCTURES *Where are you?*
What's she doing?
Can you see her?
What does she look like?

LEXIS

to steal	*nose*	departments:	*curly (hair)*
to put	*necklace*	*furniture*	
to buy	*doll*	*toy*	
to try on	*shoplifter*	*menswear*	
to look at		*hats*	
to talk (to an assistant)		*hardware*	
to wear		*food*	
		jewellery	

(see the Ideas on the opposite page)

SETTING UP
1. Ask half the class to look at the material for Student A and half the class to look at the material for Student B.
2. Tell the students to look at the instructions at the top of their material and ask:

Where do you work?	(in a department store)
What is there in every department? `	(a video camera)
What do you do?	(St.A: I'm a video controller)
	(St.B: I'm a detective)
What does a video controller/ detective do?	(St.A: he watches..., etc.)
	(St.B: he walks..., etc.)
So what are you doing?	(St.A: I'm watching...)
	(St.B: I'm walking...)

   Draw a clock on the board showing 4.00, and explain that it shows the time now. Then tell the students to look at the picture at the top of their material and ask St.A students:

What's the time on the television?	(St.A: four o'clock)
What's happening?	(St.A: there's a shoplifter)

   Get St.B students to ask St.A students for details, i.e. what exactly she's doing and what she looks like. You could ask them to do this as a telephone conversation.

3. Ask students with the same material to work in pairs and discuss which department is shown in each picture, and what the shoplifter is doing (St.A) or what they *think* she's doing (St.B).

   Use this period to check on their use of the structures and lexis and help with any problems.

4. Bring the two halves of the class together in pairs. Tell them to read the next set of instructions. Then ask:

What's the time now?	(St.B: it's ten past four)
(Change the time on the board clock to 4.10.)	
What's the problem?	(St.B: I can't see her)
What can you do?	(St.B: ask the video controller)

   Have one pair of students go through the ensuing 'telephone' conversation in front of the class to demonstrate it to the others.

   You may have to point out to St.A students that their images are *not in order,* so they have to ask the detective where he is before they can tell him what the shoplifter is doing.

   When you're sure everyone has got the idea, change the time on the board clock to 4.20 and leave them to it.

MONITORING

Don't let the students go on to the next picture until you have changed the time on the board clock. Encourage them to have a complete conversation each time, instead of just asking each other the essential questions.

The times are: 4.00, 4.10, 4.20, 4.35, 4.55, 5.25 and 5.30.

Otherwise don't intervene. Students should cope for themselves. Watch for how well they communicate (see Introduction, section 6.5).

HOMEWORK

Give the students four different times that evening, and tell them to notice and write down what each member of their family is doing at each of the times.

Ideas

PREPARATION ACTIVITIES

Present actions

Getting help   Draw the plan of a house on the board, labelling the kitchen, bathroom, etc. Next to it, write up the names of the people who live there and indicate which room each one is in. The students then imagine what each person is doing and note down their ideas.

In pairs, one student wants help to move a cupboard or to push the car, etc. and he asks his partner about what each member of the family is doing to see if they're free to help him (e.g. 'What's John doing?' 'He's having a bath.' 'OK, What's Carol doing?' 'She's watching TV.' 'That's not important. She can help me. What's Anne doing?', etc.). When they finish, they exchange roles.

Structures and lexis in the activity

Go through the names of the departments in a large store, and ask the students to give you examples of one or two things you can buy in each one (see Lexis).

To practise the verbs, write out a number of prompt cards (e.g. 'trying on a pair of shoes') and hand them out. Each student then mimes the action on his card and the others guess what he's doing *and* which department he's in.

⟫⟶

21: The department store

Meeting up   Draw a plan of, say, three floors of a department store on the board and mark in the departments. Ask the students to copy it.

The students work in pairs or small groups. Tell them they're out shopping with a friend ('Andrew', 'Janet', etc.) who is somewhere in the store. One student from each pair or group comes to you, the teacher, to find out where Janet is. He then goes back to his partner who has to guess which department she's in and what she's doing with *Yes/No* questions (e.g. 'Is she in the hardware department?' 'Is she buying a coat?'). When he's found out, he marks where she is on the plan with the time (according to his watch). Then it's his turn to come and ask you where Janet is next.

Make a list of about ten things for the person to do. The first pair to get all ten 'wins'. Follow this up by having the students use Janet's 'route' to practise 'It's (11.05). What's she doing?', etc.

FOLLOW UP   At various points in a lesson, ask the students what they *think* the members of their family and friends are doing at that precise moment.

22 INTRODUCTIONS

Notes

AIM   To practise the Present Continuous and the Simple Present.

SITUATION   The students are at a reception. They each know four of the people in the room, but not the others, so they ask each other about the people they don't know.
      The Present Continuous is used to point people out. The Simple Present is used to talk about their jobs, where they live, etc.

STRUCTURES   *Who's she?*
What's she doing?
Who's the woman sitting down and smoking?
What does she do?

LEXIS

to stand	*to hold*	*next to*	+ the professions and countries
to sit	*to show*	*behind*	on the business cards
to drink	*to pour*	*in front of*	
to smoke	*to look at*	*opposite*	
to talk			

SETTING UP   1. Ask half the class to look at the material for Student A and half the class to look at the material for Student B.
       2. Look at the picture yourself, and without pointing at anyone in it, ask:
          Who's he?   (St.A and St.B: ? ? ? ?)
          He's looking at a book.   (St.B: he's John Carter)
          Who's she?   (what's she doing?)
          She's standing next to John,
            and looking at the book too.   (St.A: she's Jo-Anne Moody)
       At this point you may wish to demonstrate the situation further by having the students get up and arrange themselves as if they were at a reception. In turn, each student asks his partner about someone in the room. He indicates the person by describing what he is doing and then goes on to ask about his job, where he lives, etc. (This type of demonstration could also be used effectively at the beginning of the activity before the students have even opened their books.)
       3. Ask students with the same material to work in pairs. They should practise describing what the people in the picture are doing, and discuss the people they already know about (job, where they live, nationality, etc.).
          Use this period to check on their use of the structures and lexis and help with any problems.
       4. Bring the two halves of the class together in pairs. Tell them to find out about the rest of the people in the picture and leave them to it.

MONITORING   A number of phrases could be added to liven up the conversation, such as 'Don't look now!', 'Shh! Not so loud!' or 'Shall I introduce you?'
      For a strong class, the reception could be set in Tokyo, for example, to

$\ggg\!\!\rightarrow$

add 'Where's she staying?' ('She's staying in the Prince Hotel.'), and they could go on to discuss whether or not the people are interesting, funny, etc.

Don't intervene. Let them cope for themselves. Instead, watch for how well they communicate (see Introduction, section 6.5).

HOMEWORK   Students write a letter to a friend enclosing snapshots of a family group. They indicate who they're writing about by saying what he or she is doing in one of the snaps and go on to say what he does, where he works, etc.

Ideas

PREPARATION
ACTIVITIES
Comparing the Present Continuous with the Simple Present

Exceptions   Draw a plan of a living room or office on the board and ask the students to copy it. Then, next to the plan, write the names of four or five people who are in the room and ask the students to imagine what each of them *usually* does at this time of the day (the time of your class). Then ask them to draw each person into the plan of the room, either doing what they usually do, or something different.

In pairs, the students discuss where each person is, what they're doing and if they usually do that at this time.

Professions   Bring in two wall charts or pictures showing people working in an office or supermarket. Divide the class in half, give one of the charts to each half and tell them to decide what each person in the picture does. The professions should *not* be related to what they are doing, so the students should also imagine why each person is doing whatever he's doing.

Bring the class together in pairs, so that all the students can see both charts. Each student then points to the people in his partner's chart one by one, asks what they do ('She's the boss.') and why they're doing what they shouldn't be doing ('Why is she typing?' 'Because the secretary is busy and her letter is urgent.').

FOLLOW UP   Arrange for two classes to meet over coffee, so that the students find themselves confronted with the 'real thing'. A difference of level between classes would not matter for this.

ROLE-PLAY
(WITH VIDEO)
Record the students being guests at a reception *without sound*. When you play the tape back, two students ask each other about the people at the reception, as in the activity.

Encourage the students to be natural and move around the room while you're filming the 'reception'. Since there is no sound, they could even improvise conversation in their native language if it helps them to relax. The scene need only be two or three minutes long.

For variety, the students could make up new, exotic names and jobs to give each other while they're watching the play-back. If your video can dub sound, record the conversation onto the sound track.

23 GREEK HOLIDAYS

Notes

AIM   To practise making and talking about plans (*What shall we do?* versus *What are you going to do?*).

SITUATION   The students are on holiday at the Mala Beach Hotel in Greece. They find out everything there is to do at the hotel and in Anavissos, a village near the hotel, and then plan the next two days of their holiday.

When they've made their plans, they discuss them with other students in the class. If they wish to alter their plans, so that they can do some things with the other students, they should do so.

STRUCTURES   *Is there a night club?*
What shall we do tomorrow?
(Let's take Greek lessons.)
What are you going to do tomorrow?
(We're going to take Greek lessons.)

LEXIS   *lounge*   *coach*
terrace   *boat trip*
excursion   *souvenir*
(guided) tour   *(traditional) costumes*
(dinner) show   *island*

SETTING UP   1. Ask half the class to look at the material for Student A and half the class to look at the material for Student B.
2. Ask the students to look at the instructions at the top of their material and ask:

Where are you?	(on holiday at the Mala Beach Hotel)
What do you want to do?	(plan the next two days)
What day is it tomorrow?	(e.g. Wednesday)
And the day after?	
What can you do on (Wednesday) and (Thursday)?	(students read out various possibilities from their material)

When they've got the idea, stop them and give them a few minutes to look through their material. Encourage them to ask you about anything they don't understand.
3. Bring the two halves of the class together in small groups of three or four, rather than pairs. Tell students with St.A material to find out about Anavissos and the excursions, using the note on their page, and tell St.B students to find out about the hotel.
4. When they've finished step 3, tell each group to start planning the next two days.
   Check briefly that they're using the structures and lexis correctly, and leave them to it.

⟫→

MONITORING   There is no reason why you should not participate as another tourist (but not as a teacher, so don't correct). Try to make the situation feel as much like a party of tourists discussing their plans in the hotel reception as possible. If one member of the group wants to opt out and do something alone on one of the days, there's no reason why he shouldn't, but in general they should try and stick together.

When they've made their plans, each group should join up with another, so that they can tell each other about them. For strong students who have finished early, suggest that they can alter their plans if they feel like doing something with another group.

Watch for how well they communicate (see Introduction, section 6.5).

HOMEWORK   Students write a postcard to a friend from the Mala Beach Hotel, explaining what it's like and what they've decided to do over the next two days.

Ideas

PREPARATION   *Making plans*
ACTIVITIES

In small groups, students make plans for:

the next lesson: (what to study, when to have a coffee break, whether or not to go to the language lab, whether to do pair or group work, a listening or reading comp., etc.)
a shop: (what to sell, how many people to employ, opening times, location, decorating, salary rates, etc.)
a nuclear attack: (where to go, transport, things to take, when to leave, how long to stay away)

Talking about plans

Once the students have made their plans (see above), regroup them so that they can tell each other about what they're going to do.

Avoiding people   Tell the students they are at a holiday camp, and list the things they can do there on the board. Then point out that two people who they don't like ('Alex and Jane') and two people who they like ('James and Sarah') are also there.

Divide the class into two halves, and ask one half to imagine everything that Alex and Jane are going to do today. The other half imagines everything James and Sarah are going to do.

Bring the two halves of the class together in pairs and tell them to make their own plans, avoiding Alex and Jane as much as possible and doing things with James and Sarah if they're doing what the students want to do ('Shall we go to the cabaret?' 'No, Alex and Jane are going to do that. What are James and Sarah going to do?', etc.).

FOLLOW UP   In groups, the students imagine they are tour operators planning the next year's holiday packages in their city. They would have to select a hotel and prepare lists of excursions and activities.

When they've finished, each group then explains their plans to the others. The students should feel free to discuss and criticize each other's plans and suggest better ideas. For homework, each student changes his plans to incorporate the ideas which have come up in this discussion, and writes the brochure for his holiday package.

Film two students sitting in the hotel reception, discussing what to do that day. They should only plan one or two things, to keep the improvisation short. Two other friends join them. They ask each other about what they're going to do and change their plans if they feel like it.

If possible, set the scene with four low armchairs and a small coffee table, and bring in typical holiday 'props' (sunglasses, camera, towels) for the students to have with them.

24 THE DINNER PARTY

Notes

AIM
To practise the use of the Present Continuous (or *going to*) for future arrangements.

SITUATION
The students decide when to have a dinner party. They want to invite six people and they have a choice of four possible dates.

Each student has a collection of notes, timetables, etc. which show what some of the guests are doing on some of the dates. Together they pool their information and decide on the best date and time to have the party.

STRUCTURES
Is John doing anything next Friday?
or *What's he doing on 12th May?*
What time does the play finish?
or *When will he be free?*

LEXIS
to have (a party)	*meeting*	dates
to move (house)	*theatre*	
to go away		
to babysit		

SETTING UP
1. Ask half the class to look at the material for Student A and half the class to look at the material for Student B.
2. Ask:

What do you want to do?	(have a dinner party)
How many people do you want to invite?	(six)
Who are they?	(Karl and Cindy Owen, etc.)
When do you want to have it?	(on 5th May or . . ., etc.)

3. Ask students with the same material to work in pairs and work out what their guests are doing on those days. Insist that they express this correctly using the Present Continuous, e.g. the invitation to a party in St.A's material should produce 'John's having a party on 6th May'.

   When they've finished, they should go through the engagements again to practise asking and answering the appropriate questions (see Structures). You may wish to suggest they use 'Is John doing anything *the Friday after next?*' instead of '*on 12th May*'.

   Use this period to check on their use of the structures and lexis and help with any problems.
4. Bring the two halves of the class together in pairs. Tell them to ask their partners about the other things their guests are doing, and find the best time for the party.

MONITORING
You may have to remind students that even if their guests have an engagement, they might not be busy all evening and could come after it.

Otherwise, don't intervene. Leave the students to cope for themselves. Watch for how well they communicate (see Introduction, section 6.5).

SOLUTION   Friday, 12th May at about 8.30. Eight o'clock is too short notice for the tennis players to change, etc. Mark could bring his brother.

HOMEWORK   Students write one or two of the invitations to the dinner party, and a note of acceptance or refusal.

Ideas

PREPARATION ACTIVITIES   *The Present Continuous (or going to) for future engagements*

Invitations   Give the students a choice of four evenings over the coming fortnight and ask them to plan (individually or in pairs) what to do on *one* of these evenings.

Each student then goes round the class asking other students to join him on his evening out ('Would you like to . . .?'). Students who are 'free' on the evening proposed could accept – or find an excuse. Students who have already accepted an invitation from another student, or who have planned something themselves for that evening would have to refuse politely and say what they're doing instead. At the end, students could compare their engagements for all four evenings.

When will you be free/back?

Fitting in   Write a dozen things which people can do in an evening on the board (see the activity itself for ideas). Tell the students to each choose seven of them, and fit them into a 'diary' for next week so that they have something booked for each day. They should note what time each engagement starts and, if possible, when it finishes (e.g. 'Tuesday: tennis 6.30–7.30').

Divide the class into pairs and tell each pair to find the *best* time for them to meet. This will inevitably be before or after their various engagements for that evening, so they should try to meet as early, and for as long as possible.

FOLLOW UP   Students plan a dinner party for the whole class for one evening this weekend or next. Insist that they treat the activity as real, with genuine complications such as having to find babysitters.

ROLE-PLAY (WITH VIDEO)   A student rings up a friend to find out when he is free to come round for supper. The student playing the friend should write a number of engagements into a diary so that he can actually consult it – and the camera can zoom in on it – during the improvisation.

Notes on camera work for telephone conversations are given in the ideas for Activity 3.

25 AT THE CINEMA

Notes

AIM To practise the Present Continuous, the Simple Present (for outlining a scenario) and *going to*.

SITUATION The students work out the plot of a film, *The Bomb*, using pictures from it and excerpts from the scenario. (They work out the plot for the first part of the film before they go on to the second part.)

In the material for the first part (pages 61 and 62 in the Student's Book), each student has two pictures and two excerpts from the scenario. The excerpts correspond to his partner's pictures, not his own. He prepares questions to ask his partner about his own pictures, using the Present Continuous (what exactly is happening and why), and uses the scenario excerpts to imagine what's happening in his partner's pictures.

The students then show each other their pictures, ask the questions they've prepared, and go on to work out the plot, using the Simple Present (what happens).

They repeat the process for the second part of the film (pages 63 and 64 in the Student's Book).

STRUCTURES *What's she doing?*
Why is he cutting the telephone line?
What are they talking about?
What happens before that?
Why does she run out of the office?
Who is she going to see?

LEXIS

to make a speech	*to cut	airline	bomb
to jump	*to hit	company	woods
to explode	to tie up	metal	*remote control
to kill	to untie	politician	*telephone line
to fly	*to catch (bus)	gangster	
to take off		pilot	strange
to land		boss	

* These words need not be pre-taught. They should become clear when they are matched with the right pictures.

SETTING UP 1. Ask half the class to look at the material for Student A (p. 61) and half the class to look at the material for Student B (p. 62).
2. Tell the students to look at the instructions at the top of their material and ask:

Where are you?	(at the cinema)
What's the film this week?	(*The Bomb*)
What's on the notice board?	(pictures from the film)
Where is the notice board?	(outside the cinema)
What happens in the film?	(Students read the second paragraph from the newspaper clip)

70

3. Ask students with the same material to work in pairs and discuss the pictures and the excerpts from the scenario, along the lines suggested in the instructions.

   Use this period to help with any problems with Lexis.
4. When they're ready, ask them to go on to task 1 at the bottom of their material. Insist that they only prepare questions they really want to know the answers to. (There should be a lot more 'Why is he...?' questions than 'What is he doing?' questions.)
5. Bring the two halves of the class together in pairs and tell them to go on with task 2 at the bottom of the material.

   A typical exchange might go as follows:

   St.B: Why is she catching a bus?
   St.A: Because some men are following her.
   St.B: Why are they following her?
   St.A: I'm not sure. She runs out of the office and they follow her.
   St.B: Ah yes, her boss and a gangster are following her.
   St.A: Why?
   St.B: Because one night she works late..., etc. What happens after that?
   St.A: She goes to a hotel.

MONITORING There is no reason why you shouldn't help students with problems while they're working out the first part of the film, but leave them to cope entirely on their own when they go on to the second part (see Introduction, section 6.5).

They could do the second part in the following lesson.

HOMEWORK 'What happens next?' is the inevitable trap of stories used for educational purposes. That fact and a good chance of the students running into extremely complicated language, are good reasons *not* to set it for homework! Instead you could have them write up short resumés for films they like, along the lines of the newspaper article in their material but a little longer.

Ideas

PREPARATION
ACTIVITIES

Outlining a scenario with the Simple Present and Present Continuous

Cartoons   Cut up a typical newspaper cartoon, about four pictures long ('Andy Capp', for example). Show the students the pictures one by one and ask them to describe what is happening in each. Then put them in order and ask them to tell you the story.

If you can duplicate a number of cartoons, have the students work in pairs, or small groups. One student has the complete cartoon, the others have it cut up into individual pictures. The first student tells the story and the others have to put the pictures in order as he tells it.

Alternatively, give the cut-up pictures to the storyteller, so that he can produce each one at the right moment to illustrate his story. Encourage the other students to ask 'Why is she...-ing?' (for the pictures) and 'Why does she...?' (for the narrative).

Sequences from most picture-through-composition books could also be used for this, or, if your students have a taste for the bizarre, use random pictures from magazines which they have to link up into a story.

⫸→

Links Write out a short, simple story and cut it into sections. Mix up the sections, divide the class into two groups and give each group half of the sections. Each group orders its sections as best it can and imagines what happens in the missing sections. Students then come together to find out whether their guesses are right or not.

Going to

Suspense Tell the class a story they all know (a fairy story, the plot of a film, etc.) but stop from time to time so that they can guess what's going to happen next. If your class is imaginative, use a story they don't know.

FOLLOW UP Bring in a film guide or newspaper which has pictorial advertisements for films. Each student should choose an advertisement for a film which he has seen and use it to explain what happens to the rest of the class. Any students who have also seen the film could help him. Encourage the other students to ask questions prompted by the advertisement (e.g. 'Who's he?', 'Why is he . . . ?' etc.).

26 LANGUAGE SCHOOL

Notes

AIM   To practise uses of *to be* in the Simple Past and the Simple Present.

SITUATION   The Sprach Schule König is a language school in Hamburg, Germany. Student A has a letter from Karen who is a student there now. Student B has a letter from Colin, an ex-student who was there in December 1981. The students use the letters to compare what the school is like now with what it was like in 1981.

STRUCTURES   *Who are/were your teachers?*
What are/were the (classrooms) like?
Is/was there a language lab?
How many students are/were in your class?
Is/was she interesting?
(Angelika) is still at the school.

LEXIS

language lab	*interesting*	*out of order*
	boring	*warm*
(un)tidy	*excellent*	*funny*
(im)patient		

SETTING UP
1. Ask half the class to look at the material for Student A and half the class to look at the material for Student B.
2. Ask:

What is the Sprach Schule König?	(a language school)
Where is it?	(in Hamburg, Germany)
Who is your letter from?	(St.A: Karen)
	(St.B: Colin)
When were they students at the school?	(St.A: she's a student now)
	(St.B: in December 1981)

3. Ask students with the same material to work in pairs. One student asks the questions suggested in the instructions below the letter, while the other scans the letter for the answers. (If your students are unfamiliar with this technique, see Note on Scanning, Introduction, section 4.)
   When they've finished, ask them to practise talking about the school together.
   Use this period to check on their use of the structures and lexis and help with any problems.
4. Bring the two halves of the class together in pairs. Tell St.A students to find out what the school was like and St.B students to find out what the school is like now.
   You could ask the students to imagine they are Colin and Karen meeting in a café in Hamburg.

⟫→

MONITORING At the end of the activity, the class should list the changes in the school, pointing out what is *still* there and what isn't there *any more*.

With a strong class you could then have the students express the changes with the Present Perfect.

Don't intervene. The students should cope by themselves. Instead, watch for how well they communicate (see Introduction, section 6.5).

HOMEWORK The students write a letter from Colin to a friend who was at the school with him in 1981. The letter should mention the meeting with Karen and outline the changes.

Ideas

PREPARATION
ACTIVITIES
There was/were and How many ... were ...?

Remembering   Prepare a tray with about twenty objects on it. Let the students look at it for two or three minutes, then take the objects off the tray and put them into a bag.

Instead of letting the students simply list what they saw, ask them specific questions about how many of each object there were. Include questions about objects which *weren't* on the tray.

Once they've got the idea, divide the class into two groups. Each group prepares its own tray to show the other half – and the questions to ask afterwards.

What is/was it like? and It's still ...

Changes   Divide the class into two groups and write the names of two hotels on the board. Tell one half that they were at the first hotel a few years ago, and the other half that they were at the second hotel at the same time. Write up points to consider on the board, such as the number of bars, the decor, the staff uniforms, etc. and ask the students to imagine what the hotels were like.

When they've finished, tell each group that they were at the *other* hotel last week, and that they should imagine what it's like now. .

Bring the two halves of the class together in pairs so that they can work out the changes in each hotel.

The same activity can be used with two areas of a city, two companies, two countries, etc.

FOLLOW UP Students could talk about their old schools or areas they used to live in, comparing what it was like with what it's like now.

In a group discussion (so that you can provide vocabulary as the need arises) ask the students where they were on the last national holiday in their country (e.g. New Year's Eve, Independence Day in America, etc.) and what it was like.

ROLE-PLAY
(WITH VIDEO)
The students act out the conversation between Colin and Karen in a café or at a party in Hamburg.

Start the improvisation by having a third student introduce Colin to Karen and start the conversation between them by pointing out that they have both been to the Sprach Schule König. Get other students to interrupt the conversation from time to time (a waiter for the café, old friends at the party).

Keep both students in shot most of the time. If you want to vary this with close-ups, try to avoid simply panning from one student to another. Instead, zoom out of a close-up until both students are back in the picture, then pan, then zoom in on the second student. That way you avoid a blurred rush of classroom between close-ups, and do not detract from what is being said.

27 THE CLASS OF '76

Notes

AIM To practise *Yes/No* questions in the Simple Past and contrast the Simple Past with the Simple Present.

SITUATION The students who graduated from Blue Hills High School in 1976 each had their plans and ambitions printed in a yearbook. One of the graduates, Donald, is writing a newsletter about the class, and he has written to some of the people who were in it for news.

Student A and Student B each have part of the yearbook and one of the letters Donald has got back. Together they find out whether or not each student did what he originally wanted to do, and what he does now.

STRUCTURES *Did John work in a bank?*   *What else did he do?*   *I (don't) think so.*
What does he do now?   *What did he do instead?*
What did he want to do?
or *What was he going to do?*

LEXIS
to get married (to someone)	*farm*	*pilot*
to get divorced	*college*	*hairdresser*
to have (a baby)	*army*	*uncle*
to become (a doctor)	*computer*	*rock group*
to study	*journalist*	*assistant manager*

SETTING UP
1. Ask half the class to look at the material for Student A and half the class to look at the material for Student B.
2. Ask:

    Where is Blue Hills High School?   (in America)
    Are the students in your book there now?   (no)
    When did they leave?   (in 1976)

  Ask St.A students:

    What did Nancy Wright want to do in 1976?   (go to college)
    Did she go to college?
    What does she do now?

Tell the students to scan the letter at the bottom of their material for the answers to the last two questions. (If they are unfamiliar with this technique, see Note on Scanning, Introduction, section 4.)

Go through the same questions with St.B students for Mary Feldmann.
3. Ask the students to tell you the names of the people (a) in their part of the yearbook and (b) in their letter, so that each half of the class is aware that the other half has the information they need.

Then put students with the *same* material together in pairs. Give them a few minutes to read through the yearbook and the letter. Encourage them not to worry about things they don't understand.

When they've finished, have them run through the questions and answers about Nancy and Mary again, and then prepare the questions about the other people to ask their partners.

4. Bring the two halves of the class together in pairs. Remind them of other questions they can ask, e.g. if the person is married or has any children (and see Structures). Then leave them to it.

MONITORING Encourage the students to ask one question at a time, and give precise answers to their partner's questions, instead of simply reading off all the information about each graduate at once.

Otherwise don't intervene. The students should cope by themselves. Watch for how well they communicate (see Introduction, section 6.5).

HOMEWORK The students write the newsletter, perhaps imagining that they too had been in the class.

Ideas

REPARATION ACTIVITIES

Yes/No questions in the Simple Past

Checking   In pairs, the students write out lists of things for their partners to do. The situation could be that of a wife who will be home late writing a note to her husband, a boss to an employee, someone to a friend who is going into town, etc.

When they've finished, the students exchange lists. Each one reads his partner's list and decides what he 'did' or 'didn't do'. If he didn't do something, he must decide why he didn't, and not use the same excuse twice. The students then return the lists to their partners and role-play the conversation when the wife, boss or friend gets back.

If there is a risk of confusion with the Present Perfect, have the students back-date their lists, so that the things on them should have been done 'last week' or 'yesterday', etc.

Yes/No questions in the Simple Past, going to

Intentions   The students ask each other what they are going to do that evening or next weekend, and note the answers. In the next class, after the evening or weekend, they ask each other if they did what they had intended to do.

Holidays   The students imagine they are at the beginning of their last holiday and write a postcard about where they are and what they plan to do. Get them to date their postcards.

In pairs, they then exchange postcards. Each pair then role-plays the conversation, now that they are both 'back from holiday', asking if they did or didn't do what they had planned. If a student didn't do something, he must be able to explain why not. For things he did do, he could add details of what exactly happened and what it was like.

FOLLOW UP The students discuss what they wanted to do when they left school, and what actually happened to them.

ROLE-PLAY (WITH VIDEO) The students discuss the people in their own school photographs. If these prove difficult to obtain, use an appropriate picture from a magazine and have the students invent the ambitions (and fates) of the people in it.

Notes for camera work in this type of situation are given with the Role-play ideas for Activity 4.

28 THE SEMINAR

Notes

AIM   To practise *Wh* questions in the Simple Past.

SITUATION   The activity is set in Singapore. St.A was supposed to go to a seminar at the Java Hotel, but he went out with a friend instead. Unfortunately, his boss has asked him to write a report on the seminar.

       St.B was at the seminar, so St.A can ask him for all the relevant details about it. When they've finished talking about the seminar, St.B asks St.A about his evening out.

STRUCTURES   *What did you do (after that)?*
What time did it start?
Who was the speaker?
How long was the film?
What was it about/like?

LEXIS

to have (dinner)	*discussion*	*baked*	*wonderful*	*instead*
to talk (about)	*idea*	*roast*	*excellent*	
	theatre		*interesting*	
report	*discotheque*			
seminar	*crab*			
speaker	*a good time*			

SETTING UP
1. Ask half the class to look at the material for Student A and half the class to look at the material for Student B.
2. Ask St.A students:

Where did your boss send you last week?	(to a seminar at the Java Hotel)
Did you go?	(no)
Why not?	(I went out ..., etc.)
But what's the problem?	(my boss wants a report ..., etc.)

Ask St.B students:

Where did you go last week?	(to the seminar)
What information have you got about it?	(the programme with notes)

3. (a) Ask all the students to turn to page 10 in their books. Use the article on the 3rd October seminar to run through the questions they will need (see Structures) e.g. 'First Mr Appleby talked about ...' should produce the question 'What happened first?' or 'What did you do first?'

    (b) Have the students turn back to their material and give them a few minutes to go through it, perhaps working in pairs with the *same* material. Encourage them to ask you about anything they don't understand.

    Note: You could do steps (a) and (b) in reverse order.

4. Bring the class together in pairs. Point out that you are the St.A students' boss, and the future of their job depends on an accurate, detailed knowledge of last week's seminar. Then leave them to it.

MONITORING   You may have to point out that St.B students should ask their partners about
their evening out, once they've finished talking about the seminar.
Otherwise, don't intervene. The students should cope for themselves. Watch
for how well they communicate (see Introduction, section 6.5).
When they've finished, ask St.A students about the seminar, and St.B
students about the evening out to see what details they have missed.

HOMEWORK   The students write a report on the seminar using the 3rd October report as
a guide.

Ideas

PREPARATION   *Wh questions in the Simple Past*
ACTIVITIES
Ordering   Students role-play ordering a meal in groups of three or four (the menu
could be written out on the board). A waiter (you or another student) then brings
them the bill and they work out what each of them owes, asking each other about
what they had and consulting the menu to find out how much it costs.

Cheques   In pairs or small groups, students imagine they have a joint bank
account. Each student writes out three or four imaginary cheques (to shops,
restaurants, 'cash', etc.) and dates each one with a date from last month.
The students then make a list together of the amounts they each spent,
as if it was their bank statement for last month, but they don't show each
other their cheques. They then question each other about each amount,
asking where the person who wrote the cheque went, or what he did, etc.
and comment/criticize ('£80 for a new dress!!').

Touring   In pairs, one student imagines he went on an organized tour of
a city (get brochures from a local tourist office to help him), while the other
imagines he went out with a few friends. Both students have a few minutes
to note what they did and what they thought of it. They then discuss and
compare their evenings out.
The same type of process could be used to compare whether it would
be more fun or better value for money to take a package holiday to
somewhere or to go there independently.

What ... about?

Since this appears frequently in the activity, your students may need some
preliminary practice.
– Phrases like 'What was the film/book about?' and 'What did you talk about?'
can be brought into a general conversation about weekend activities, etc.
– With a monolingual class, you could give each student a simple newspaper
article in their native language, and ask them to tell you what it's about
(perhaps from the headline only). A strong class could go on to ask and answer
questions about what actually happened.

FOLLOW UP   You could ask the students to write a report giving details about what
happened in the English lesson (over a week if the lessons are short). They
might even include comments and criticism ...
Every time a student has missed a lesson, he should ask the others (not
you) about what happened in the class he missed.

⟫→

28: *The seminar*

The students improvise the situation in the activity.

Start a close-up of the note from the boss pinned to a notice board. A student takes it down and reads it. Zoom out slowly at this point to show the student reading it and another student standing next to him, consulting something else on the board. The first student starts a conversation with the other along these lines:

St.A: Oh no!

St.B: What's the matter?

St.A: The boss wants a report on the seminar last week. (etc.)

The students should limit their conversation to half a dozen questions each. You might suggest the phrase 'Can we talk more about this later? I'm (seeing a customer) in a moment.' for them to use when they want to stop the conversation.

29 CAR HIRE

Notes

AIM   To practise using the Past Continuous; describing people.

SITUATION   A customer of Quick Car Hire (Student B) has had problems trying to rent a car. When he arrived at the agency, hardly anyone was working, and no-one made any effort to serve him. The customer decides to complain and phones the manager.

The manager (Student A) has had complaints before, and would like to stop this happening again, but before he can do so, he needs to know exactly what each of his employees was doing.

Note: The situation described in the letter (St.A) is different from the one shown in St.B's material.

STRUCTURES   *What was he doing?*
Who was reading a newspaper?
What did he look like?

LEXIS

to decide	*manager*	*short*	
to talk (about)	*person/people*	*long*	
to count	*nobody*	*curly*	*hair*
to wear (glasses)		*straight*	
to laugh	*another*	*dark*	
		light	

Note: Each person can be described by hair style and whether or not he or she wears glasses.

SETTING UP
1. Ask half the class to look at the material for Student A and half the class to look at the material for Student B.
2. Ask St.B students:
   - What did you want to do yesterday?   (rent a car)
   - Where did you go?   (to Quick Car Hire)
   - What was the problem?   (nobody helped me ..., etc.)

   Ask St.A students:
   - What do you do?   (I'm the manager ..., etc.)
   - What did you get yesterday?   (a letter from a customer)
   - Why did he write you a letter?   (he was very angry)
3. Ask a student with St.A material to keep his book open while the rest of the class shut theirs. Ask this student to scan the letter and read aloud what each person in the office was doing. Get the other students to pretend they are the office staff, and do what he describes in front of the class.

   When the students have completed the tableau, ask two other students to be the manager and the customer. The customer describes the situation to the manager. Insist that the manager asks what each person looks like, and 'guesses' which student it is when he is told.

   (For correct use of the *Past* Continuous, the students in the tableau

81

should go back to their seats before the customer starts talking to the manager. You could also have the manager leave the room while the students make the tableau, so that he never actually sees it.)

4. Bring the class together in pairs and leave them to it. Point out that the manager should note what each of his employees was doing.

MONITORING *Note:* There is one person in St.B's picture who doesn't work for Quick Car Hire.
Don't intervene. The students should cope for themselves. Instead, watch for how well they communicate (see Introduction, section 6.5).

HOMEWORK The students write a letter to the manager about the situation on St.B's page.

Ideas

PREPARATION
ACTIVITIES *The Past Continuous*

Linking moments Ask one student to write down in detail what he did on the previous day between, say, 2 and 6 p.m. He should give a precise time to each action. Ask the rest of the students to imagine they met him during this period. Tell them to each choose the precise time when they met him.

One by one, the students then tell this time to the original student, and he tells them what he was doing then, without any of the other students overhearing. Once everyone has done this, the students go round asking each other:

St.A: What time did you see him?
St.B: I saw him at (2.45).
St.A: What was he doing?
St.B: He was (reading a book).

At the end, the students reconstruct what the original student did (Simple Past) between 2 and 6 p.m.

The Past Continuous and physical descriptions

Memories Divide the class up into pairs or small groups, and give one student in each pair or group a picture showing a number of people doing different things. This student lets the others see it for about ten seconds. He then describes each of the people in the picture, and the others have to say what each person was doing.

To reinforce the use of the past, you could tell the students that the scene they have just seen happened yesterday, for example.

TV The students think of several TV programmes they have seen recently and note down images they remember from them. Each student then says when he saw the programme and describes the image (the people in it and what they were doing). The others try to guess which programme he's talking about.

FOLLOW UP – Students share memories they have of poor service in shops, or when someone came in at a bad moment.
– Students describe advertisements they have liked or disliked. This could bring up some interesting points if they describe advertisements which are appearing in magazines, etc. at the moment (Present Continuous), or TV advertisements (Simple Past or Present).

ROLE-PLAY
(WITH VIDEO)

The students improvise arriving at a party. When the video is played back, each student describes what the others were doing when he arrived.

Start with just one student, the host, in the room. (He could be arranging bottles, tidying the flat, etc.) The other students come in one by one, without knocking, at, say, thirty second intervals. As they arrive, they immediately start doing something – the first ones could help the host put the finishing touches to the flat, later ones talk, get drinks, smoke, put on 'records', etc. They should behave exactly as if they're at a real party – not doing the same things for too long, and not paying particular attention to new arrivals – so that the scene alters before each new student comes in.

When all the students have come in, send the 'host' out (for more wine?) so that he can 'arrive' too.

As you're playing the video back, each student describes what the others were doing at the moment he arrived.

30 PUBLIC LIVES

Notes

AIM   To practise talking about people's lives with the Simple Past.

SITUATION   Each student has an incomplete set of notes about the life of a (dead) person, and has to ask his partner for the missing information. His partner has an article about the person which he scans for the answers.

St.A has notes for a woman called Marta Lenska, St.B has notes for a man called Charles Morton.

STRUCTURES   *When was (Charles Morton) born?*
Where did he die?
What was Changes *about?*
How long did he live in England?

LEXIS   *to live*   *to marry*   *journalist*   *problem*   dates (e.g. 1906)
to die   *to send*   *engineer*   *photograph*
to be born   *to study*   *medicine*   *article*

SETTING UP   1. Ask half the class to look at the material for Student A and half the class to look at the material for Student B.
2. Ask:
    Who are your notes about?   (St.A: Marta Lenska)
    What's the problem?   (St.B: Charles Morton)
                                 (a lot of information is missing)
3. Ask students with the same material to work in pairs and decide what questions they need to ask to find out about the missing information.

When they've finished, get them to practise scanning the article at the bottom of the page. One student in each pair should use the notes as prompts to ask questions while the other scans the article for the answers (although St.A's notes are about Marta Lenska, they can be used to prompt the same type of questions about Charles Morton, e.g. 'When was he born?', etc.).

If your students are unfamiliar with scanning, see Note on Scanning, Introduction, section 4.

Use this period to check on their use of the structures and lexis, and help with any problems.
4. Bring the two halves of the class together in pairs, tell them to complete their notes and then leave them to it.

MONITORING   When they've finished, have a class discussion about what happened in the students' countries, and in the world in general, during the lives of these two people. You could have them link these events with the people's lives, e.g. 'Marta left Poland after World War Two'.

Don't intervene. The students should cope for themselves. Instead, watch for how well they communicate (see Introduction, section 6.5).

84

Ask the students to write up the article from their notes, using the article in their material as a model.

Ideas

Talking about dates of birth, death, etc.

Famous names   Prepare a list of ten statements about a famous person, starting with (approximate) dates of birth, death, places where he or she studied, lived or worked, etc., before going on to more obvious clues involving what he or she did in adult life.

Read the statements out to the students one by one and have them try to guess who the person is before you get to the end of your list.

Students can then prepare their own lists about famous people of their choice to try out on the other students. If you insist that they follow your original ordering of the statements ('Question 1: date of birth', etc.) you could write up question prompts on the board so they have to ask for each statement.

Dynasties   Write short histories of various members of a family over, say, four generations. These histories could be extremely short, specifying only dates of birth, death, who they married, what they did and what they were like. You could connect the fortunes of each member of the family to the history of the students' country at the time, or let your imagination go wild with eccentrics, dissolute sons, daughters who start multinational companies, etc. Write the history of each member of the family on a separate card.

In class, write the names of all the members of the family on the board. Give one card to each student and ask the class to go round asking each other about the family. Once they've done this, the students can work in groups to decide who was whose father and mother (working from clues such as dates of birth and death, where they lived when they were young, etc.) and make up a family tree. They should then prepare a short summary of the rise and fall (?) of the family's fortunes.

– Students could talk about the lives of their grandparents and other relatives, perhaps concentrating on periods which tie them into their country's history (e.g. 'What did she do in the war?') and explaining what life was like then ('They had/didn't have . . .').
– Each student could be asked to prepare a report on an important (dead) person in his country. While he's reading his report to the class, the other students take notes. If you make it clear from the start that each student should leave some dates and places out of the report, you will be able to encourage the other students to ask for the missing information after the speech.

Students improvise a guided tour around their home town, much along the lines suggested in the video improvisation for Activity 11.

This time, however, the student(s) playing the tour operator(s) would concentrate on statues, and the birth places or homes of famous people.

31   BUSINESS LETTERS

Notes

AIM   To practise telling people what (not) to do; to teach simple letter writing technique.

SITUATION   Each student has two business letters. Each letter involves (a) thanking for a previous letter (b) placing an order (c) enclosing a cheque.

Each student has one letter which is only partially correct. He uses it to correct his second letter as far as he can, then asks his partner for help in correcting the rest of each letter. St.A has the correct model for the heading and closing. St.B has the correct model for the body of the letter.

STRUCTURES   *You mustn't* | *write 'Dear Mr'. You must write 'Dear Sir'.*
Don't |
Can I put the date below the signature?

LEXIS   *to write*   *in the top right hand corner*
to put   *below*
to sign   *above*
to leave (margins/spaces between paragraphs)

SETTING UP
1. Ask half the class to look at the material for Student A and half the class to look at the material for Student B.
2. Ask:

Who did Mr Knight/Mrs Drew write to?	(Carter's Mail Order)
What did he/she ask for?	(their catalogue)
Did they send it to him/her?	(yes)
When did they send it?	(St.A: on 10th February)
	(St.B: on 25th May)
Did he/she write back?	(yes)
When?	(St.A: on 23rd February)
	(St.B: on 1st June)

3. Ask students with the same material to work in pairs and read the letter carefully. Go around the class checking that they understand the contents of the letter.

When they've finished, ask them to read the second letter. Ask them the same type of questions as in step 2 (above) for this letter, and have them read it carefully. Again, check that they understand the contents.
4. Ask them to correct the second letter by comparing it with the first. Insist that they find a way of explaining the corrections to each other.

Use this period to check on their use of the structures and lexis and help with any problems.
5. Bring the two halves of the class together in pairs. Point out that the students should show each other their letters and discuss how to correct them. Suggest that they try to explain the corrections without pointing at what they're talking about at all. Then leave them to it.

MONITORING   You might suggest that once they have learned from their partner how to correct the first letter, they should explain how to correct the second letter

86

themselves to check that they have understood their partner's instructions.

Don't intervene. The students should cope by themselves. Instead, watch for how well they communicate (see Introduction, section 6.5).

Students write out or type all four letters correctly.

Ideas

Must (telling people what to do)

The doctor Discuss and then write on the board a list of reasons why someone might (a) be overweight or (b) sleep badly (among the obvious reasons, you might include being worried or unhappy about something).

Ask the class to form two groups. Using the list on the board for reference, one group discusses what the doctor might advise, and the other group works out the daily life of someone who has these problems, (e.g. the time he drinks his last cup of coffee in the evening).

Bring the class together in pairs. Students from the first group are the doctors, students from the second are patients. The doctor asks the patient about his daily life and then advises him.

Marriage contracts In some parts of the United States, marriage partners can 'negotiate' their vows before the wedding ceremony. Introduce the idea to the students and ask them to invent their own, ideal marriage contract.

Explaining how to organize and write letters, forms, etc.

Cheques Draw a blank cheque on the board, of the type most of the students are familiar with, and have the students explain to you how to fill it in.

Then draw a blank cheque with an unfamiliar format (British or American if you're teaching abroad) or, if you have a multinational class, have the students draw blank cheques of the type used in their home countries. The students then have to ask you (or each other) how to fill it in.

Encourage them to make intelligent guesses for their questions, e.g. 'Do I put the date here?', not always 'What must I put here?'

—Have the students explain how business letters are written in their countries.
—Find out about their hobbies (pets, gardening, sports, models, etc.) and ask them to give you advice, e.g. if the hobby is gardening, you could ask how deep you must plant trees. If you have a strong class, encourage them to distinguish between what you must, should and can do.
—You could also discuss etiquette rules in the students' home countries.

The students demonstrate how to organize a business letter.

Cut up a business letter into its component parts, i.e. the date, your address, salutation, etc. Spread these parts around a blank sheet of paper on a table. During the improvisation, the students pick up and discuss each part, and then place it in the correct position on the blank sheet.

Since this is a demonstration, make sure the letter is always somewhere in the picture, and zoom in on it from time to time. When you play the tape back, the viewers must always be able to see what is being talked about.

At the end of the improvisation, zoom out to the original picture.

32 BUSINESS TRIP

Notes

AIM
To practise talking about obligation with *have (got) to ...* and contrast it with *I'd like to ...*

SITUATION
Both students are going on business trips.

Part 1: Each student has a list of things to do during the three days before he leaves. Some of the things he has to do, others are more flexible (*I'd like to ...*), and since he's still working, he can only do them at lunch time or after work.

Each student works out a timetable and then tries to find a free hour to see his partner. He will almost certainly have to alter his timetable, moving things he doesn't *have* to do at a certain time to another day.

Part 2: Each student asks the other about the regulations in the country he's going to. This is essentially an exercise in converting 'official' language (*It is required ...*, etc.) into everyday language (*You have to ...*).

STRUCTURES
What are you doing (on Tuesday evening)?
Do you have to go to the hairdresser's then?
I'd like to go home for a shower.

LEXIS
to be (at home by ...)   *safety belt*   *visa*
to collect (car)   *motorway*
to pack   *medical care*

SETTING UP
Part 1

1. Ask half the class to look at the material for Student A and half the class to look at the material for Student B.
2. Ask:
   What are you doing next Thursday?   (going on a business trip)
   When can you do the things on your list?   (12.30–2.00, + after 6.00 Monday–Wednesday)
3. Have students with the same material work in pairs, and decide which things they have to do, and which they'd like to do.

   They should go on to work out a timetable for the three days. It might help them organize their work if you draw a structure for the timetable on the board for them to copy, like this:

	M	T	W
lunch			
evening			

88

When they have finished, have them practise making an appointment
with each other.

Use this period to check that they're using the structures and lexis
correctly.

4. Bring the two halves of the class together, and leave them to it.

Part 2

1. Practise the lexis for regulations with the students by asking them about
   regulations in their own country. Use each of the headings in the regulations
   as the prompt for one question, (e.g. 'Visas' produces 'Do you have to
   have a visa?').
2. Ask:

Where are you going on the trip?	(St.A: Paris)
	(St.B: London)
What have you got?	(St.A: the regulations for the UK)
	(St.B: the regulations for France)
What do you need?	(St.A: the regulations for France)
	(St.B: the regulations for the UK)

3. Point out that *You are required . . .* and *It is compulsory . . .* mean *You
   have to . . .* You could also discuss official language in general, and how
   rarely it's actually spoken. Then give the students a few minutes to
   'translate' the regulations in their material, perhaps working in pairs.
4. Bring the two halves of the class together in pairs and leave them to it.

MONITORING   In part 1, insist that students find the *best* time (see Solution).

Don't intervene. The students should cope by themselves. Instead, watch
for how well they communicate (see Introduction, section 6.5).

SOLUTION   *Mon. 6–7*: but St.A has to collect his car another day, and it leaves no margins.
Tues. 6–7: again possible, but can St.B really get home for a shower and
then to the theatre in 30 minutes?
Wed. lunchtime: the best time. St.B has to get his traveller's cheques on
Tuesday, and go to the hairdresser's on Monday, but the meeting won't be
rushed at all.

HOMEWORK   Students write to a foreign friend who is coming to visit them about the
regulations in their country. They could also mention when they will be free
to do things with this friend – and why they won't be free at other times
('I have to work on Monday, but I arrive home at 5.00, so . . .').

Ideas

REPARATION
ACTIVITIES

Talking about regulations with have (got) to

Alternative societies   Draw two islands on the board and give them names.
Tell the class that twenty people, including children, have gone to each
island to set up their own societies. Write up a list of topics on the board
(e.g. voting, school, tax, work sharing), divide the class into two groups
and assign each group to one island. Each group works out the laws for
their society.

When they're ready, bring the class together in small groups and tell the
students to find out what is the same for each society and what is different.   ⟫→

Talking about obligations

Jobs   Each student thinks of a job and writes down the daily routine of
someone who does it (Simple Present). He then reads this out to the class.
The other students ask if he's obliged to do what he describes, e.g.:
St.A: I arrive at work at nine o'clock.
St.B: Do you have to arrive at nine?
St.A: No, I don't. I can arrive at ten.
The class then try to guess what the job is.

FOLLOW UP   The students could discuss other laws in their own countries, or procedures
such as getting a work permit or a loan on a house. They could also ask
you if the same applies in your home country. Provide vocabulary as the need
arises.
A similar discussion could take place comparing religions.

ROLE-PLAY   Students improvise telephoning different embassies to find out about the
(WITH VIDEO)   regulations in different countries.

33 AU PAIRS

Notes

AIM
To practise talking about obligations in the present with *have (got) to* and in the past with *had to*.

SITUATION
Diana (St.A's material) is an au pair girl with the Moretti family in Rome. Marleen (St.B's material) used to be an au pair with the Citto family, but she has left to become an English teacher. Diana is unhappy working for the Morettis, so when she sees an advertisement for a job with the Citto family, she asks Marleen about it.

    The students discuss why Diana wants to leave her job and whether the job with the Cittos would suit her, considering what Marleen had to do when she was there. They also discuss what Marleen's new job is like.

STRUCTURES
I like (getting up late).
What's the room like?
Do you have to . . .?
Did you have to . . .?

LEXIS
to do the | *housework*   *independent*   *ugly*
           | *washing*   *bad*   *shy*
to get . . . from school   *funny*
to take . . . to school   *lovely*   *quite (nice)*
to practise   *rarely*

SETTING UP
1. Ask half the class to look at the material for Student A and half the class to look at the material for Student B.
2. Ask St.A students:
    What does Diana do?   (she's an au pair)
    Who does she work for?   (the Moretti family)
    What does she want to do?   (leave her job)
Tell St.A students to work together in pairs. Ask them to scan the letter and make the notes suggested in their material. Students will probably find it easier to list everything she has to do first and then go back and find out if she likes doing them.
Ask St.B students:
    What did Marleen do last year?   (she was an au pair)
    Who did she work for?   (the Citto family)
Tell St.B students to work together in pairs. Ask them to scan the letter and list the things Marleeen had to do and what the Citto family was like.
    If your students are unfamiliar with the technique of scanning, see Note on Scanning, Introduction, section 4.
3. When they've finished, ask St.A students about the advertisement Diana saw, and check that they are aware that Marleen has worked for the Cittos.
    Then tell them to prepare the questions to ask their partner about Marleen's old job.

                                                          ⟫→

Talk to the St.B students about what an English teacher has to do.
Use this period to check on their use of the structures and lexis and help with any problems.

4. Bring the two halves of the class together in pairs. Suggest that the St.B students start things off by asking why Diana doesn't like her job, and leave them to it.

The activity works best if the students do it as a role-play with Diana and Marleen meeting in a coffee bar, for example.

MONITORING   Don't intervene. The students should cope by themselves. Instead, watch for how well they communicate (see Introduction, section 6.5).

HOMEWORK   Students think about a summer job they have had and then write about it to a friend who is thinking of doing the same job.

Ideas

PREPARATION   *Talking about obligation in the past with had to*
ACTIVITIES

Jobs   Adapt the activity on jobs suggested in the Preparation Activities for Activity 32 by asking the students to think of jobs they've had in the past, like summer jobs.

Alternatively, ask one student to describe (briefly) the first job he had after he left school. Ask the rest of the class to imagine what that kind of job involves, (e.g. 'A postman gets up early. He drives a van.'), and then ask the student whether his job was like that ('Did you have to get up early? Did you drive a van?'). Continue with another student or have the students continue independently in small groups.

Disasters   Disastrous events such as getting a huge tax bill, being caught in an airport strike or without petrol, or flooding your neighbour's apartment, can all be treated as follows:

Prepare two cards for each event. On one card write a short story about someone who has had a disaster, e.g. 'Mrs Pike never paid her taxes, and last summer she got an enormous tax bill. She didn't have to sell her house, but . . .', etc. On another card, describe what *can* happen to people in this situation, e.g. 'Some people have to pay enormous tax bills. Sometimes they have to sell their house or find a new job. Sometimes . . .', etc.

The students work in pairs with one of the cards each. The student with the 'story' card describes the disaster (i.e. the first sentence *only* in the above example) and his partner, with the 'possible consequences' card, asks about what the people in the story had to do (e.g. St.B: 'Did Mrs Pike have to sell her house?' St.A: 'No she didn't, but she had to (sell her car).', etc.).

Alibis   A variation on 'alibis' goes as follows:
Explain to your students that there was a party at your house last Saturday evening. Everyone in the class was invited but no-one arrived on time. Everyone was four to five hours late. Give the students time to prepare their excuses.

Each student then makes his excuse and the rest of the class ask questions to check that he *had* to do what he was doing. The class then decides whether the excuse is convincing or not.

33: Au pairs

FOLLOW UP   Students could discuss what they had to do at school or when they were
teenagers living at home. Summer or temporary jobs could also be discussed.

ROLE-PLAY   The students improvise the conversation between Diana and Marleen (you
(WITH VIDEO)   could change the names if you're working with male students).
    Write out the advertisement for the job with the Cittos and pin it to a notice
board, together with other small advertisements. Start with a close-up of it,
and then continue along the lines suggested for the video improvisation for
Activity 28.

34 SECOND OPINIONS

Notes

AIM
To practise using question tags to check facts, contrasted with *Wh* and *Yes/No* questions.

SITUATION
The students are journalists. They each have to interview someone, and have a list of statements about the person which they *think* are true. Since each student also has an article about the person his partner has to interview, they can check these statements with each other. They go on to ask the *Wh* questions at the bottom of their lists.

STRUCTURES
Tag endings:
isn't he?
wasn't he?   *What does she do in her spare time?*
doesn't he?   *Does he like interviews?*
didn't she?
hasn't she?

LEXIS
to be in (a film)	*businessman*	*Scottish*
to play (a part)	*actor*	*relaxed*
to go | *jogging*	*organization*	*friendly*
horse riding	*a company*	
	law	*until*
solicitor	*comedy series*	
(deputy) mayor		

SETTING UP
1. Ask half the class to look at the material for Student A and half the class to look at the material for Student B.
2. Ask:

    What do you do?   (I'm a journalist)
    Who do you have to interview?   (St.A: Reg Fisher)
                                             (St.B: Carol Roberts)
    Why?   (St.A: he's in a play at Evesham)
                                             (St.B: she's the new mayor)

    Are you sure your interview
       notes are correct?   (no)
    How can you check them?   (ask my partner)
    Why?   (he's got an article about
                                                Carol/Reg)
3. Ask students with the same material to work in pairs and prepare the questions they will have to ask their partners later.
    They should also skim through the article in their material to get a general idea of it.
    Use this period to check on their use of the structures and lexis and help with any problems.
4. Bring the two halves of the class together in pairs and leave them to it.

94

MONITORING   At the end of the activity, discuss which of the statements in their notes were wrong and what the correct statements are. (*Note:* one statement in each list has no answer in the corresponding article.)

Don't intervene. The students should cope by themselves. Instead, watch for how well they communicate (see Introduction, section 6.5).

HOMEWORK   Students could prepare a series of interview questions based on their corrected notes, or write an interview about themselves or someone they know, using the article given in their material as a model.

Ideas

PREPARATION   *Question tags*
ACTIVITIES

Triangles (checking uncertain information)   Prepare a questionnaire with five or six questions on it, e.g. if the students have (got) a walkman, what kind of perfume they wear, if they were at the school last year, etc. Tell each student to ask one or two other students these questions and note the answers (St.A: 'Have you got a walkman, John?' St.B: 'Yes, I have.'). Then tell the students to ask each other about the people they've just been talking to (St.C: 'Has John got a walkman?' St.A: 'Yes, he has.'). Finally, the students ask each other if what they've been told is true (St.C: 'You've got a walkman, haven't you, John?' St.B: 'Yes, that's right.').

Once the students get the idea, do the activity again with different questions, and tell the students that this time they can lie when they're talking about other people, but they must tell the truth about themselves.

Memories   Divide the class into groups of three or four. Tell each group to learn as much as they can about a cousin (or other relative) of one member of the group (likes, dislikes, age, etc.). Students should not take notes.

When they've finished, help them forget half of what they've just heard by doing something different for 10–20 minutes. Then put the students back in their groups. Tell them they have to look after this cousin for a week-end and must decide what to do with him/her. Remind them to use question tags for what they remember ('She likes playing tennis, doesn't she?') and ordinary questions for what they didn't ask or have forgotten.

Interruptions   Write your own simple article about a recent news event. Also write a list of statements giving supplementary information about the people and places mentioned in the article. Give this list to the students (or give one statement to each student), and encourage them to interrupt you while you're reading the article:

Teacher: He met Mr Carter in . . .
Student: Mr Carter was the American President, wasn't he?

Follow this up by asking students to prepare their own news stories. Before each student reads his story to the others, he should tell them the subject(s) of his story and give them a few minutes to write down things they remember about that subject. Students then interrupt each other's stories.

FOLLOW UP   Question tags are often useful in group conversations because they can be used to direct the conversation and encourage silent members of the group to join in.

⟫→

Use the activity material to demonstrate how an interviewer does his 'homework' before the interview, so that he can use question tags to direct the conversation and encourage his guest to go into detail on particular topics (see the articles).

Give the class a discussion topic (e.g. houses), and select a chairman. Ask everyone to write their name and one simple statement about the topic on a piece of paper. Suggest that the statement begins with *I*, e.g. 'I've got a large house' or 'I don't like flats'. Everyone then gives their paper to the chairman so he can bring each student into the conversation one by one ('Julie, you don't like flats, do you? . . .').

Keep these conversations short – one or two sentences from each student – and have lots of them with a different chairman each time.

35 INTERVIEWS

Notes

AIM To practise the use of the Present Perfect with *ever*, and the Simple Past.

SITUATION Shepherd Films is looking for an assistant photographer for an expedition to Brazil. Each student has the CV and interview notes for one applicant.

 The students work out and discuss how well each applicant meets the requirements of the job, and then go on to discuss which one is best for the job.

STRUCTURES *Has (Helen) ever lived in a hot country?*
How long did she live there?
Can she speak Portuguese?
How well can she speak it?

Note: An understanding of *must* and *should* will help students decide which job requirements are essential and which are not.

LEXIS *to go on an expedition*　*assistant photographer*　dates (e.g. 1959)
to take photographs　*curriculum vitae*
to look after　*application*
to join　*applicant*
to climb　*game reserve*
to have experience of
to do a | *degree in*　'the job includes ...'
　　　　 | *course in*

SETTING UP 1. Ask half the class to look at the material for Student A, and half the class to look at the material for Student B.
2. Ask:
 What is Shepherd Films?　(a film company)
 Who is it looking for?　(an assistant photographer)
 Why?　(for an expedition to Brazil)
 What experience do you need
　for the job?　(Students use both the advertisement and the note to find the answers)

 Who are Jerome and Helen?　(applicants)
 What information have you
　got about them?　(a CV, a photo and notes)
3. Ask students with the *same* material to work in pairs, and find out how well their applicant meets the job requirements. One student could ask the questions (using the advertisement and the note) while the other finds the answers. Encourage students to follow up with extra questions like 'When exactly did he ...?'

 Use this period to help with language problems. Encourage students to ask you about what they don't understand.

 Students with tense problems could start by discussing what the applicant has done in his life and when he did it, before they go on to compare the applicant's experience with the job requirements.

⟫→

97

4. When all the students are ready, bring the two halves of the class together in pairs and leave them to it.

A variation would be to have the students work in groups of three. One student would play Sue Reynolds, using only the advertisement and the note, while the other students each defend one of the applicants. (Don't do step 3 of Setting Up in this case.)

MONITORING

Don't intervene. Students should cope entirely on their own. Instead, watch for how well they communicate (see Introduction, section 6.5).

HOMEWORK

Students write a report for their boss on the applicant of their choice, giving reasons as to why they have chosen this applicant.

Ideas

PREPARATION
ACTIVITIES

Have you (ever) . . .?

Types   Discuss with the students the things which different types of people do, eat, wear, etc. You could for example compare a stockbroker, a tramp, a film star, a local thug . . .

The students then ask each other (a) if they do these things ('Do you . . .?') and if not, (b) if they have ever done them ('Have you ever . . .?'), and if so, (c) why and (d) what it was like.

The 'sexism' activity described in the Ideas for Activity 19 could be adopted along the same lines.

Fantasies   Each student writes down a few things he'd like to do but has never done. These could range from visiting exotic places and trying out new sports, cars, etc. to fantasies of being extremely rude to one's boss or writing graffiti on advertisements. Students then find out if anyone in the class has actually done these things, or knows someone who has, and what it was like.

Students could do the same for jobs which they have never done but are curious about (working in a shop, market, farm, etc.).

Job experience   Bring a job advertisement from a newspaper into class. The requirements for the job should not be too specific.

Discuss with the students the kind of experience which a person in that kind of job might have. Then ask them to work in small groups and write the CV for someone who they think would be perfect for the job. The class then discusses each group's candidate and selects the best one (candidates with too many qualifications/experience should be rejected – they would probably leave the job after a short time).

FOLLOW UP

Students write their own CVs, which they bring into class. They then use these in one of the following ways:
– Students mention what they have done in their lives and the other students ask them for details ('When?' 'How long?', etc.).
– Students briefly explain their jobs to the class. The class imagines the qualifications, experience and abilities that job might require and asks about them ('Have you (ever) . . .?'). For third person practice, students could exchange and scan each other's CVs for the answers.

ROLE-PLAY
(WITH VIDEO)
Have the students invent their own 'market survey' type questionnaires incorporating 'Have you ever' questions (e.g. 'Have you ever used Flash?'). Notes for camera work in this context are given with the Role-play ideas for Activity 19.

36 SOAP OPERA

Notes

AIM   To practise the use of the Present Perfect for recent events.

SITUATION   The students are watching an episode of a soap opera, *Los Angeles*. Student A has missed half of the episode, so he asks Student B to bring him up to date on the story.

      Student A's pictures show the situation at the end of the last episode, so he can ask specific questions (see Structures). Student B's pictures show what has happened in the present episode.

STRUCTURES   *What has happened to (Tom)?*
Has Billy found a job yet?

LEXIS

to miss	*to catch fire*	*tractor*
to steal	*to die*	*television serial*
to have | *a baby*	*to break down (car)*	*ranch*
| *problems*	*to be pregnant*	*episode*
		computer

SETTING UP
1. Ask half the class to look at the material for Student A and half the class to look at the material for Student B.
2. Have a brief discussion about TV series in general and go through the eight characters in the activity. You could encourage students to speculate on what each character is like (e.g. honest, ambitious, etc.).
   Then ask:

What's on TV at the moment?	(an episode of *Los Angeles*)
Have you watched all the episode?	(St.A: no, I've missed half)
	(St.B: yes)
What are your pictures about?	(St.A: the situation at the end of the last episode)
	(St.B: what's happened in this episode)

3. Ask students with the same material to work in pairs.
   St.A students should work out the situation shown in each of the pictures and think of the questions they'll be asking their partner later (see Structures).
   If they finish early, suggest they predict what they think will happen to each character.
   St.B students work out what has happened to each character in the current episode. One student could ask questions about each character while the other finds the answers.
   Use this period to help with language problems and check on the students' use of the structures and lexis.
4. Bring the class together in pairs and leave them to it.

MONITORING   Don't intervene. The students should cope entirely on their own. Instead, watch for how well they communicate (see Introduction, section 6.5).

The students write letters to a friend telling them what has happened recently in their families.

The students write a resumé of the latest events in a television serial which they actually watch. They could go on to include personal criticisms of the series, predictions for the next episode, etc.

Ideas

The Present Perfect with the Simple Past

Faces   Draw four or five simple faces on the board. Give each of them names and tell the class what each one wanted to do or wanted to happen two months ago. By changing the faces' mouths to a smile or a frown you can get the class to tell you if these things have or haven't happened.

Once they've got the idea, ask them to imagine other things each character wanted to do. Write their ideas on the board. Then divide the class into two groups. Allocate half the characters to one group, and the other half to the second group, and ask each group to decide whether these things have happened to their characters or not. Encourage them to discuss how each thing has happened or why it hasn't happened.

When they're ready, bring the two halves of the class together in pairs so that the students can ask each other about the characters they haven't decided anything for.

Check lists   In pairs students write a list of things for someone to do. These could be from a boss to his secretary, wife to husband (or vice versa), chef to waiter, parent to babysitter or neighbour, etc. Pairs then exchange lists and decide whether they have or haven't done the things on the list they've been given, with explanations.

Sightseeing   The class plans two alternative schedules for a day's sightseeing tour of their city. Suggest that the tours are for specific groups of people, such as football supporters or art students, to stimulate ideas. The two schedules should be written up on the board.

Tell the students it's three o'clock on the day of the tour. Divide them into two groups. Each group works with one of the schedules and imagines what they have and haven't done so far (some things may have taken longer than expected) – Present Perfect – and things that happened to each of them in each place (someone lost their ticket/money (at the museum), was bored/interested/ill, etc.) – Simple Past.

The two halves of the class then meet and ask each other about their tours and if they have gone as planned.

Students discuss what has happened recently in their families or to people they know at work.

37 POLITICS

Notes

AIM To contrast the use of the Present Perfect (for periods which are not finished) with the use of the Simple Past (for periods which are finished).

THE PRACTICE WORKSHEET

(*Note:* The class should do the worksheet and the activity on different days.)

The worksheet gives students practice in the lexis, structures and skills needed for the main activity.

Half the class look at the worksheet for Student A and half the class look at the worksheet for Student B. Exercise 2 is the same for both students. Exercises 1 and 3 involve information exchange between them.

EXERCISE 1 *Structures:* Income tax | *went up to 19% in 1980.*
| *has gone up to 22% since 1980.*

       Lexis: *to go up/down*   *inflation*
             to stay (at)   *income tax*
             per cent (%)   *unemployment*
                                    graph
                                      population

Teaching points: Use the income tax graph to teach and practise the structures and lexis before you ask the students to fill in the missing words in the paragraph on the right.

In pairs, each student should ask his partner for the information he needs, e.g. 'What happened to inflation in 1979?' or 'Has unemployment gone up this year?' rather than simply letting his partner dictate the graph.

EXERCISE 2 *Structures:* *The Green government increased inflation.*
                   The White government has reduced inflation.

       Lexis: *to be in government*   *political party*
              to increase
              to reduce

Teaching points: The exercise refers to the graphs in exercise 1.

The percentages refer to the *overall* results of each government. Students may find this easier to understand if you ask them to draw a vertical line on each graph dividing the period of the Green government ('78–'81) from the White period ('81–?).

EXERCISE 3 *Structures:* *The Green government built 42 hospitals.*
                   The White government | *has bought ten fighter planes.*
                                           | *bought ten fighter planes in 1984.*

       Lexis: *to cut (spending)*   *public spending*
              to nationalize   *defence spending*

army   industry   steel
war   subsidy
fighter plane

Teaching points: Ask students with St.A material to categorize what the
Green government did under the three headings of public spending, defence
spending and industry. St.B students do the same for the White government.
When the students are ready, bring them together in pairs so they can
find out about their partner's government.
Encourage students to use both *It has bought* and *It bought . . . in 198–*
for the White government.

FURTHER   Discuss the students' own government(s) performance(s), or ask them to invent
PRACTICE   details (the best/worst performance they can imagine?).

THE MAIN ACTIVITY

(*Note:* The class should do the worksheet and the activity on different days.)

SITUATION   The activity takes place on Lentz, a (fictional) island. The students compare
the performances of two governments in Lentz, one which went out of power
several years ago, and one which is still in power. They then discuss the
problems Lentz is currently facing, what the election promises of a new
government should be, and which party to vote for.

STRUCTURES   (See notes for the worksheet, exercises 1, 2 and 3.)
AND LEXIS   also: *election*
to vote
to be elected

SETTING UP   1. Ask half the class to look at the material for Student A and half the class
to look at the material for Student B.
2. Ask:
   What is Lentz?   (an island in the Indian Ocean)
   What are the two parties in Lentz?   (Sky and Wave)
   Which party is in government now?   (Wave – since 1982)
     How long?
   Which party was in government before
     that? How long?   (Sky – 4 years)
   What information have you got about
     the Sky/Wave governments?   (an article in the *Lentz Times*)
   When was it written?   (St.A: a few days ago)
                                           (St.B: in 1982)

   What has the Wave government done
     about industry?   (students scan the articles
   What did the Sky government do about   for answers)
     industry?
   If your students are unfamiliar with scanning, see Note on Scanning,
   Introduction, section 4.)
3. Ask students with the *same* material to work in pairs, and work out the
answers to the question at the top of their material. One student could
ask the questions while the other scans for the answers.
   If the students with St.B material are confused about why their article

103

uses the Present Perfect, remind them of when it was written (i.e. 1982 while the Sky government was still in power).

Check that the students do not just read the answers. All the questions and answers in the St.B group should be in the Simple Past; in the St.A group they should be in the Present Perfect. If the St.A group wants to use the Simple Past, their questions should be precise, like 'When did they ... ?', 'What happened in (1984)?'

Use this period to help with language problems. Encourage students to ask you about what they don't understand.

4. Bring the two halves of the class together in pairs, and tell them to find out about, and compare, the performances of the two governments. Then leave them to it.

MONITORING   Don't intervene. The students should cope by themselves. Instead, watch for how well they communicate (see Introduction, section 6.5).

HOMEWORK   If they are sufficiently informed, students could write an article comparing the performances of two governments in their own country.

If not, they could write an 'editorial' for the *Lentz Times*, supporting one of the parties. The article should convince, so encourage them to stress favourable evidence and suppress anything unfavourable.

38 GETTING IN TOUCH

Notes

AIM To practise the use of the Present Perfect Continuous, with the Simple Present and the Simple Past.

SITUATION The students bring each other up to date about four people. When they find out how much these people have changed, they ask how long they've been living differently and why they've changed. The reasons for these changes are not *always* clear cut.

STRUCTURE *Does Sue still live in London?*
How long has she been living there?
Why did she go to Manchester?
He's leaving (next year).

Note: the activity uses *for* and *ago*, but not *since* (*since* could be introduced if you ask the class to work out the actual dates of each event during stage 3 of Setting Up).

LEXIS

to take (classes)	*to get* | *divorced*	*spare time*
to save (money)	| *married*	
to have | *(a baby)*	| *a job*	*vegetarian*
| *(an accident)*	*to hurt (your back)*	*overweight*
to go on a diet		*slim*

SETTING UP

1. Ask half the class to look at the material for Student A and half the class to look at the material for Student B.

    Stronger students should be given the B material. At times they'll have to think around a question, (e.g. not 'Why did she start being slim?' but 'What happened?').

2. Ask:

Where does Peter/Sue live?	(St.A: he lives in Nigeria)
	(St.B: she lives in Manchester)
What do you want to know?	(how long he/she's been living there and why he/she went there)
How can you find out?	(from the letters)
When were your letters written?	(three years ago and a few weeks ago)
So how long has Peter/Sue been living in Nigeria/Manchester?	(The students read the letters and work out the answers)

3. Ask students with the same material to work in pairs and work out the rest of the answers. One student could ask the questions ('How long has Sue . . .?', etc.) while the other finds the answers.

    When they've finished, ask them to read the information about the two people at the bottom of their material and work out the questions they will ask their partners later.

    Use this period to check on their use of the structures and lexis and help with any problems.

⫸→

4. When all the students are ready, bring the two halves of the class together in pairs. Check that they understand that their partner can bring them up to date on the people at the bottom of their material, then leave them to it.

MONITORING
Don't intervene. The students should cope by themselves. Instead, watch for how well they communicate (see Introduction, section 6.5).

HOMEWORK
The students write letters to a friend who hasn't seen them for five or ten years, bringing him up to date about themselves and their family.

Ideas

PREPARATION
ACTIVITIES

The Present Perfect Continuous

Experience   Prepare, or have the students prepare, a questionnaire about activities which the students all probably do or have done, e.g. learning English, smoking, driving, etc.

The students then find out who in the class has the most experience in each area by asking (a) 'Do you (live in London)?' or 'Can you (type)?', followed by (b) 'How long have you been (able to type)?' if the answer is *yes*, or 'Have you ever ...?' and 'How long did you ...?' if the answer is *no*.

The doctor   Adapt the 'doctor' idea for Activity 31, by telling the student who is playing the doctor to follow up each of his questions with a 'How long have you been ...?' question. The doctor can then modify his advice on the basis of his patient's answer. For example, if the patient has been smoking a lot for a long time, the doctor could suggest cutting down, whereas if the patient has just started smoking, the doctor should insist that he stops immediately.

Welfare   Set the situation that the local council has a limited number of flats at very low rent which they will give to the most needy applicants. Tell the students to imagine they are applying for the flats, and note down, on a piece of paper, imaginary facts which they feel will give them a chance to obtain one of the flats (e.g. how long they've been unemployed/living with relations/on the housing list/in prison, etc.).

When they've finished, collect their pieces of paper, and do something completely different for about twenty minutes to help them forget what they've written.

Then give one student in the class one of the notes (not his own). This student then checks if the student who wrote the note was trying to cheat the local council by asking him how long he has been doing each thing, and then comparing his answers with what he had written on his note. Give the next note to a different student, and so on.

At the end, the students who have not been caught 'cheating' get the flats.

The same principle could be used with different contexts, e.g. job applications or lying about your identity to the police.

FOLLOW UP
The students discuss what they do, their interests, hobbies and plans for the future, and find out how long they've been doing them and why they started.

38:   Getting in touch

The students role-play two of the characters in the activity meeting each other at a party or in the street. Point out that they haven't met for several years and the meeting is a complete surprise for both of them.

Begin the improvisation with a shot of one of the students talking to a third student. The other student then walks up to them and taps the first student on the shoulder. After the first few moments of surprise ('Sue! What are you doing here?') the third student excuses himself and leaves the other two to talk.

Alternatively the two students could each be with friends and notice each other at adjoining tables in a restaurant or in a cinema queue.

39 THE NENEBRIDGE REPORTER

Notes

AIM Revision of most of the structures covered in *Think Twice*, including some Passive.

SITUATION Working in two teams*, the students prepare rival radio news programmes. One team works with the A material, the other works with the B material.

Each team selects at least two of the three photographs in their material, and imagines the news stories behind them. They should go into a fair amount of detail† and write their ideas down in note form.

The two teams then meet, and try to find out as much as they can about each other's stories. They should not give away more than they're actually asked for – after all, they're preparing *rival* news programmes.

When they're ready, each team gives their news programme using all the stories. The programmes are then compared to find which important details each team missed or got wrong (if any) and which presentation is the most effective.

* The teams should have no more than three or four students in each, and make sure there are an even number of teams so that the teams can be paired.

† Throughout the activity the students can consult *The Nenebridge Reporter* (pages 94–5 in the Student's Book). The articles in this newspaper cover essentially the same subjects as the students' photographs, so that the students can get ideas for details from them.

STRUCTURES (Passive) *How many people were hurt?*
How long were they trapped?

SETTING UP 1. Ask all the students to look at *The Nenebridge Reporter* (pages 94–5 in the Student's Book).

Use the articles to give the students practice in the skills and language they will need later in the activity.
   (a) *Details:* Ask various comprehension questions for each article and have the students scan for the answers (if your students are unfamiliar with this technique, see Note on Scanning, Introduction, section 4).
   (b) *Questioning:* Allocate one of the articles to each student (if you have a large class, the students could work in groups). Ask the students to work out all the questions which the journalist who wrote their article had to ask. Use this period to check on their use of structures and lexis, and help with any problems.
   (c) *Note-taking:* Throughout the activity, students should work with notes, rather than writing everything out. When they give the programme, this will produce a more spontaneous delivery, and give you a better idea of their command of English.

Reserve two of the articles to give them practice with the skill.

For the first article, write a list of points such as 'place', 'time', 'number killed', etc. on the board, and give them a time limit of two or three minutes to note down the corresponding information. When the time limit is up, have them close their books and give you the answers in complete sentences.

For the second article, simply tell them to note as many details as they can, and again give them a time limit.

If they've never done any note-taking, try the ideas suggested in the Introduction, section 6.2, first.

2. (You could do this stage in the following lesson.)

Divide the class into teams (see Situation, above).

Ask half the teams to look at the material for Student A and the other half to look at the material for Student B, and tell them to begin task 1 in their instructions.

MONITORING   Help the students to go on from one task to the next, if they don't automatically do so.

There is no reason why you should not provide vocabulary if your students ask for it. Encourage the students to correct each other, rather than ask you for correction.

Encourage them to take notes rather than writing everything out in full (see Setting Up).

When they're ready to start planning how to present the programme (task 3), add a touch of urgency to the situation by telling them they have only ten more minutes before they're 'on the air'. When the ten minutes are up, stop all the students from working whether they're ready or not, and have the first team give its programme.

You may wish to record these on a cassette-recorder, so that you can go through them with the class in the following lesson.

(and see Role-play ideas, below)

Ideas

PREPARATION
ACTIVITIES   *Talking about news stories*

Summaries   Bring in, or ask the students to bring in, newspapers in the students' native language(s). Give one article to each student, and ask him to summarize the news story. If you wish to give the summary a context, tell him that you are a foreigner visiting his country and you don't understand.

You could go on to have each student invent (not translate) an English headline for the article. You could also encourage the other students to ask for details about the story.

You could record TV and radio news bulletins and treat them in much the same way.

Headlines   Write two headlines on the board, and ask the students to imagine the kind of details which would be in the story following each headline (see the articles in the activity itself for ideas). Note the points on the board as the students mention them (e.g. 'place', 'how many hurt', etc.).

Then divide the class into two groups and ask each group to imagine the story for one of the headlines. When they've finished, bring the two halves of the class together in pairs, so that they can ask about each other's stories.

⫸→

FOLLOW UP   The students discuss their personal experience of events like the ones described in the articles.

The students write their own newspaper about recent local events.

ROLE-PLAY
(WITH VIDEO)   The students present the news they've prepared during the activity in the form of a five-minute television news broadcast.

Encourage them to vary their presentation, perhaps by converting one or more of the stories into interviews, including 'on location' reports, a rundown of the main headlines at the beginning and end of the broadcast, the weather, etc.

Use the 'Pause' button on your camera or video tape recorder to move from the 'news desk' to an interview or an 'on location' report. If you pan the camera between each of these, the result will be confusing.